# Clojure Web Development Essentials

Develop your own web application with the effective use of the Clojure programming language

**Ryan Baldwin**

[PACKT] open source*

PUBLISHING

community experience distilled

BIRMINGHAM - MUMBAI

# Clojure Web Development Essentials

First published: February 2015

Production reference: 1180215

Published by Packt Publishing Ltd.
Livery Place
35 Livery Street
Birmingham B3 2PB, UK.

ISBN 978-1-78439-222-2

www.packtpub.com

# Credits

**Author**
Ryan Baldwin

**Reviewers**
Eduardo Díaz
Shu Wang
Nate West
Daniel Ziltener

**Commissioning Editor**
Usha Iyer

**Acquisition Editor**
Neha Nagwekar

**Content Development Editor**
Rohit Kumar Singh

**Technical Editors**
Prajakta Mhatre
Rohith Rajan

**Copy Editors**
Pranjali Chury
Veena Mukundan
Vikrant Phadke

**Project Coordinator**
Mary Alex

**Proofreaders**
Ting Baker
Maria Gould

**Indexer**
Mariammal Chettiyar

**Graphics**
Disha Haria
Abhinash Sahu

**Production Coordinator**
Manu Joseph

**Cover Work**
Manu Joseph

# About the Author

**Ryan Baldwin** is a theatre major turned computer science geek. Hailing from the prairies of Western Canada, Ryan has been developing software on a wide array of platforms and technologies since 2001. Once, he wrote a crazy system application that compiled XSD Schema Docs into XAML forms that performed two-way binding with underlying XML documents in .NET WPF. Why? Because it had to be done. Another time, he worked on a project that mashed many social networks into one gigantic thing that essentially allowed users to find out all of their indirect connections. It was eventually shelved.

In 2012, he relocated to Toronto, where he works with the University Health Network, developing systems and tools that facilitate patient information exchange. You can often find him wearing headphones and jittering in coffee shops.

I'd like to thank Packt for giving me this opportunity and Dmitri Sotnikov for pushing me to do it. Without either of you, I probably would have gotten a lot more sleep and a lot less experience out of life. I'd also like to thank Chris Kay Fraser, without whose support and vegan brownies I would have never had the confidence to pursue such a project. I'd finally like to thank my family, friends, colleagues, and anybody else who interacted with me over these past several months; I'll buy you a "thank you" beer for putting up with me. All my reviewers who took the time to read, recheck, and provide essential feedback, I owe all of you at least a pitcher of beer (hit me up next time you're in Toronto). And, of course, I'd like to thank you, dear readers; without you, none of this would have happened. I am both humbled and terrified of you.

# About the Reviewers

**Eduardo Díaz** is a Java developer, with experience particularly in web development. He has been interested in finding new programming paradigms and languages since he started developing software.

Clojure (and functional programming with Clojure) caught Eduardo's attention as an excellent mixture of a very unique paradigm and a pragmatic approach to programming. He has used it to build a data collection platform for several high-traffic sites, similar to Google Analytics. Clojure was an excellent choice for him, because it minimized errors and development time.

> Writing this book was an incredible idea! More developers need to know the power of Clojure and how it can make their lives better. Thank you Ryan Baldwin and everyone involved in making this book happen!

**Nate West** is a polyglot web developer based in Nashville, Tennessee. While he has yet to meet a language he doesn't like, he found his home in the land of Lisp. As a developer at Blue Box, he gets paid to write in Ruby. When not learning new languages, he enjoys hanging out with his wife, playing with his dog, philosophizing over a cup of coffee, and mentoring at Nashville Software School.

**Daniel Ziltener** was born in the canton of Bern in Switzerland. He started programming at the age of 10 and acquired broad general knowledge about programming and software engineering, including desktop and web development and the programming languages such as Java, C++, Scala, Clojure, and Scheme. He started his studies in computer science at the University of Bern in 2012. Since then, he has worked as a Clojure software developer at the university's historical institute.

I'd like to thank the awesome Clojure community for all the great libraries and their support, especially in #Clojure, while I was learning Clojure a few years ago—it's been since 1.3! I'd also like to thank my employer for regularly giving me time off to review this book. You all really enabled me to become a Clojure pro.

# www.PacktPub.com

## Support files, eBooks, discount offers, and more

For support files and downloads related to your book, please visit www.PacktPub.com.

Did you know that Packt offers eBook versions of every book published, with PDF and ePub files available? You can upgrade to the eBook version at www.PacktPub. com and as a print book customer, you are entitled to a discount on the eBook copy. Get in touch with us at service@packtpub.com for more details.

At www.PacktPub.com, you can also read a collection of free technical articles, sign up for a range of free newsletters and receive exclusive discounts and offers on Packt books and eBooks.

https://www2.packtpub.com/books/subscription/packtlib

Do you need instant solutions to your IT questions? PacktLib is Packt's online digital book library. Here, you can search, access, and read Packt's entire library of books.

### Why subscribe?

- Fully searchable across every book published by Packt
- Copy and paste, print, and bookmark content
- On demand and accessible via a web browser

### Free access for Packt account holders

If you have an account with Packt at www.PacktPub.com, you can use this to access PacktLib today and view 9 entirely free books. Simply use your login credentials for immediate access.

# Table of Contents

# Preface

Clojure is a beautiful, concise language, and its adoption for web applications is ready and about to explode. In *Clojure Web Development Essentials*, you will learn how to build a Clojure web application from scratch using the Leiningen build tool and the Luminus application template. We'll start by creating a simple example application in the first few pages of the first chapter, and build on that application with each subsequent chapter. We'll cover URL routing, template rendering, database connectivity, form validation, and everything else we need to build a typical web app. By the end of this book, you'll have the knowledge required to venture into the world of web development, and you'll be able to use your skills for the betterment of the Internet.

## What this book covers

*Chapter 1*, *Getting Started with Luminus*, guides you through creating a new project using the Luminus application template. We'll then dive into what was generated, what the out-of-the-box project dependencies are, and the general file structure of a Luminus web app.

*Chapter 2*, *Ring and the Ring Server*, describes the core technologies driving our application, and shows you how to use the development web server.

*Chapter 3*, *Logging*, demonstrates configuration of some basic logging and the Clojure logging library, Timbre.

*Chapter 4*, *URL Routing and Template Rendering*, starts to dive into the important part of web applications. It shows you how to handle incoming requests using Compojure, and how to render web pages using the Selmer templating engine. We'll also create a sign-up form for our application.

*Chapter 5*, *Handling Form Input*, teaches you how to validate form data and report form validation errors back to the user.

*Chapter 6, Testing in Clojure,* is a quick tour of automated testing and its use in Clojure.

*Chapter 7, Getting Started with the Database,* is the first of three chapters covering database management and interactivity. We'll set up our application's database, and you will learn how to manage your database schema using the Migratus Leiningen plug. Then we will store the form input created in the fifth chapter using YeSQL.

*Chapter 8, Reading Data from the Database,* continues exploring database interactivity by teaching you how to retrieve data from the database using YeSQL. We'll then create a couple of new web pages that list the most recently added items in our database.

*Chapter 9, Database Transactions,* gives us a brief overview of what database transactions are. We'll then create a form that transactionally inserts data into multiple tables.

*Chapter 10, Sessions and Cookies,* demonstrates how sessions and cookies are managed and maintained in Noir. We'll then create an authentication form for our application, and save a cookie in the user's browser to remember their username the next time they log in.

*Chapter 11, Environment Configuration and Deployment,* guides us through abstracting our environment configuration (such as database connectivity) and describes a few common ways by which we can deploy our application.

*Appendix, Using Korma – a Clojure DSL for SQL,* covers the modification of the YeSQL model layers to use Korma, a native Clojure Domain Specific Language that can be used to interact with the database if you're not keen on using raw SQL.

# What you need for this book

First and foremost, you must be familiar with the Clojure programming language. You'll also need to install the Leiningen build tool. Familiarity with basic web technology is also valuable.

# Who this book is for

This book targets software developers who are already using Clojure but want to use their skill set for web applications. Very little of this book does any fancy frontend development, and most of it focuses on server-side development. If you're primarily a frontend developer, or have never heard of Clojure, this book is precisely *not* what you are looking for.

# Conventions

In this book, you will find a number of styles of text that distinguish between different kinds of information. Here are some examples of these styles and explanations of their meanings.

Code words in text, database table names, folder names, filenames, file extensions, pathnames, dummy URLs, user input, and Twitter handles are shown as follows: "We can include other contexts through the use of the include directive."

A block of code is set as follows:

```
:dependencies [[org.clojure/clojure "1.6.0"]
               [lib-noir "0.9.4"]
               [ring-server "0.3.1"]
               [selmer "0.7.2"]
               [com.taoensso/timbre "3.3.1"]
               [com.taoensso/tower "3.0.2"]
```

When we wish to draw your attention to a particular part of a code block, the relevant lines or items are set in bold:

```
:ring {:handler hipstr.handler/app
  :init hipstr.handler/init
  :destroy  hipstr.handler/destroy
  :open-browser? false}
```

Any command-line input or output is written as follows:

```
# lein ring server-headless
```

**New terms** and **important words** are shown in bold. Words that you see on the screen, in menus or dialog boxes for example, appear in the text like this: "clicking the **Next** button moves you to the next screen."

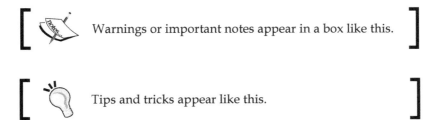

> [ Warnings or important notes appear in a box like this. ]

> [ Tips and tricks appear like this. ]

# Reader feedback

Feedback from our readers is always welcome. Let us know what you think about this book—what you liked or may have disliked. Reader feedback is important for us to develop titles that you really get the most out of.

To send us general feedback, simply send an e-mail to feedback@packtpub.com, and mention the book's title via the subject of your message.

If there is a topic that you have expertise in and you are interested in either writing or contributing to a book, see our author guide at www.packtpub.com/authors.

# Customer support

Now that you are the proud owner of a Packt book, we have a number of things to help you to get the most from your purchase.

# Downloading the example code

You can download the example code files from your account at http://www.packtpub.com for all the Packt Publishing books you have purchased. If you purchased this book elsewhere, you can visit http://www.packtpub.com/support and register to have the files e-mailed directly to you.

# Errata

Although we have taken every care to ensure the accuracy of our content, mistakes do happen. If you find a mistake in one of our books—maybe a mistake in the text or the code—we would be grateful if you could report this to us. By doing so, you can save other readers from frustration and help us improve subsequent versions of this book. If you find any errata, please report them by visiting http://www.packtpub.com/submit-errata, selecting your book, clicking on the **Errata Submission Form** link, and entering the details of your errata. Once your errata are verified, your submission will be accepted and the errata will be uploaded to our website or added to any list of existing errata under the Errata section of that title. Any existing errata can be viewed by selecting your title from http://www.packtpub.com/support.

# Piracy

Piracy of copyrighted material on the Internet is an ongoing problem across all media. At Packt, we take the protection of our copyright and licenses very seriously. If you come across any illegal copies of our works in any form on the Internet, please provide us with the location address or website name immediately so that we can pursue a remedy.

Please contact us at `copyright@packtpub.com` with a link to the suspected pirated material.

We appreciate your help in protecting our authors and our ability to bring you valuable content.

# Questions

If you have a problem with any aspect of this book, you can contact us at `questions@packtpub.com`, and we will do our best to address the problem.

# 1

# Getting Started with Luminus

Ah, getting started! This chapter introduces you to the foundations of **Clojure** web development using **Luminus**, a popular web application template for **Leiningen**. In this chapter, you will:

- Generate a new web application using the Luminus Leiningen template
- Get an introduction to the popular libraries, which Luminus uses to handle the various aspects of a web application, and what those libraries do
- Get an overview of the directory structure generated by Luminus
- Learn how to fire up the web application on your development machine

In this chapter, we'll create a new web application called **hipstr**, an application that will help us track our vinyl collection and endow us with obscure credibility. We'll build this application with each subsequent chapter by creating our own route handlers, interacting with a database, authenticating users, validating form input, and reading/writing cookies. By the end of this book, we'll know the Clojure web basics well enough that we'll be wearing plaid shirts and sipping bourbon aged in casks from a place nobody's ever heard of.

# Leiningen

Our project will rely heavily on Leiningen, a build and task tool for Clojure. Leiningen allows us to easily maintain our application's dependencies, assists us in common tasks such as database migrations, running tests, producing binaries (**jars** and **wars**), and a plethora of other things. Leiningen is akin to Java's build tool Maven (`http://maven.apache.org`), and Ruby's Rake (`http://github.com/jimweirich/rake`). As Leiningen's web page (`http://leiningen.org`) concisely puts it: *for automating Clojure projects without setting your hair on fire.*

If you haven't already installed Leiningen 2.x, head over to `http://leiningen.org/#install` and follow the four simple instructions. It will take just 60 seconds, and the world of Clojure will become your oyster.

 After you've installed Leiningen, you'll have access to a new command in your terminal, `lein`. Invoking this command will invoke Leiningen.

# Using Leiningen

The basic makeup of a Leiningen task can be summarized as follows:

```
# lein $TASK $TASK_ARGUMENTS
```

In the preceding shell pseudo-command, we invoke Leiningen using its binary. The `lein $TASK` argument is the Leiningen task we want to execute (such as `install`, `jar`, etc.), and `$TASK_ARGUMENTS` is any information required for that task to do its job, including additional subtasks and the arguments for a given subtask. You can see a full list of the available tasks in Leiningen by executing the following command:

```
# lein --help
```

You can also view the help content for a specific Leiningen task by executing the following command:

```
# lein help $TASK
```

You can use these commands whenever you need to know how to do something in Leiningen.

# Generating the application

Leiningen can generate an application skeleton (or scaffolding) from a plethora of different *templates*. There's a template for nearly everything such as `clojurescript` projects, web applications (of course), and much more.

To generate a new application, we use the `new` Leiningen task whose basic syntax is as follows:

```
# lein new [$TEMPLATE_NAME] $PROJECT_NAME
```

The new task expects, at a minimum, a name for the project ($PROJECT_NAME). Optionally, we can provide a specific template to use ($TEMPLATE_NAME). If we don't specify a template, then lein will use the default template, which is a general template for developing libraries.

For our project we'll use the Luminus template, an excellent template for web applications. Luminus generates a project and wires in the libraries to support pretty much every aspect of web development including sessions, cookies, route handling, and template rendering.

> At the time of this writing, the Luminus template was at version 1.16.7. To ensure the code examples in this book work, you can force Leiningen to use a specific version of Luminus by modifying Leiningen's profiles.clj file (typically found in your home directory, in a folder called .lein) to include the specific version of Luminus. For example:
>
> ```
> :user {:plugins [[luminus/lein-template "1.16.7"]]}
> ```
>
> This modification will ensure that version 1.16.7 of the Luminus template is used when generating a Luminus-based application.

Just try the following command:

```
# lein new luminus hipstr
>> Generating a lovely new luminus project named hipstr…
```

> **Downloading the example code**
>
> You can download the example code files for all Packt books you have purchased from your account at http://www.PacktPub.com. If you purchased this book elsewhere, you can visit http://www.PacktPub.com/support and register to have the files e-mailed directly to you.

The preceding command will generate a fully runnable application in a directory called hipstr. You can run the application by using cd hipstr to enter into the hipstr directory and then execute the following command:

```
# lein ring server
>>(Retrieving im/chit/cronj/1.0.1/cronj-1.0.1.pom from clojars)
>>…a whole bunch of Retrieving…
>>…and other output…
>>Started server on port 3000
```

In the preceding command line, the `lein ring server` command updates our class path with the dependencies required to compile and run the app. It then launches the development server (an embedded Jetty server) and starts serving on port 3000. Lastly, it launches our default web browser and navigates to the root page.

In the preceding example, `ring` is the Leiningen task, and `server` is the `ring` subtask. You can view a full list of `ring` subtasks by entering the `lein help ring` command in your terminal.

The subsequent output of `lein ring server` is a series of debug statements that lets us know what the heck is going on during the startup process. Any generated exceptions or problems that occur while attempting to launch the application will be emitted as part of this output.

## Getting help

If anything doesn't go as planned, or you're stumped and confused, feel free to check the Luminus documentation at `http://www.luminusweb.net`. You can also get some help from people in the Luminus community (`https://groups.google.com/forum/?fromgroups#!forum/luminusweb`) or the Ring community (`https://groups.google.com/forum/?fromgroups#!forum/ring-clojure`). Of course, there's always the Clojure group on Google Groups (`https://groups.google.com/forum/#!forum/clojure`).

# Dependencies of the app

The Luminus template provides good starting defaults for a typical web application by using popular libraries. It also configures common tasks (such as logging) and provides a few default route handlers (URL handlers).

Taking a peek at the generated project.clj file, we see all the dependencies included by the `luminus` template. At the time of writing, the project.clj file produced the following dependencies:

```
:dependencies [[org.clojure/clojure "1.6.0"]
               [lib-noir "0.9.4"]
               [ring-server "0.3.1"]
               [selmer "0.7.2"]
               [com.taoensso/timbre "3.3.1"]
               [com.taoensso/tower "3.0.2"]
               [markdown-clj "0.9.55"
```

```
        :exclusions [com.keminglabs/cljx]]
[environ "1.0.0"]
[im.chit/cronj "1.4.2"]
[noir-exception "0.2.2"]
[prone "0.6.0"]]
```

 Luminus is a popular and active project, and is constantly getting better. Between now and the time this book goes to press and you purchasing one for each of your friends and yourself, it's possible that the template will have changed. At the time of writing, version 1.16.7 of the luminus template was used. If you used a more recent version your results may vary.

The first dependency should look familiar (if not, then this book isn't for you… yet). The rest, however, might appear to be a mystery. I'll spare you the effort of searching it online and break it down for you.

- `lib-noir`: This contains a slough of useful utilities to create web applications using the Ring framework, such as routing, redirections, static resources, password hashing, file uploads, sessions and cookies, and so on. It's the work horse for much of the plumbing common to all web applications. Visit the following website: `https://github.com/noir-clojure/lib-noir`.

- `ring-server`: This is a bit of an omnibus library, encompassing several other Ring-related libraries. Ring is a web application library, which acts as an abstraction between our web application (`hipstr`) and the underlying web server or servlet container. You can think of it as something akin to Java's **Servlet API** (which Ring fulfills), Python's **WSGI**, or Ruby's **Rack**. Ring Server, by contrast, is a library that starts a web server capable of serving a Ring handler. We'll get into more detail in *Chapter 2, Ring and the Ring Server*. To get more information about Ring Server, visit: `https://github.com/weavejester/ring-server`

- `selmer`: This is an HTML template rendering a library modeled after the ubiquitous **Django** framework. Selmer allows us to generate dynamic pages, script loops and conditional rendering, extend other Selmer templates, and so on. We'll talk more about Selmer in *Chapter 4, URL Routing and Template Rendering*. To get more information on `selmer` , visit: `https://github.com/yogthos/Selmer`

- `timbre`: Timbre is a pure Clojure logging library. It's pretty much like every other logging library on the planet, complete with somewhat confusing configuration. We'll cover Logging in *Chapter 3, Logging*. You can also visit `https://github.com/ptaoussanis/timbre`, to get more information on Timbre.

- tower: This is similar to its sibling timbre, and is a pure Clojure library that provides support for internationalization and localization. You can refer to https://github.com/ptaoussanis/tower.

- markdown-clj: This is a simple library that allows us to compile markdown to html. For more information, you can visit https://github.com/yogthos/markdown-clj.

- environ: This allows us to create different application configurations for different environments (think development versus production). We'll work with environ in *Chapter 11, Environment Configuration and Deployment.*

- cronj: This is a simple, straightforward library for creating cron-like scheduled tasks. To know more about cronj, visit https://github.com/zcaudate/cronj.

- noir-exception: This provides prettified, rendered, exception stacks in the browser as well as to log files. The noir-exception library highlights your application's namespaces in their own color, easily separating your *called* code from the rest of the first and third party Clojure libs.

- prone: This produces the most amazing exception reporting output you might have ever seen. (https://github.com/magnars/prone).

# Luminus file structure

The luminus template generates web applications using a fairly typical directory structure. However, it also produces a number of Clojure namespaces that can cause a bit of confusion if you're brand new to Clojure web development. You can either open the project using your favorite Clojure editor, or do the following from the terminal:

```
# find . -print | sed -e 's;[^/]*/;|____;g;s;____|; |;g'
```

The preceding command line is a nasty thing to eyeball and type. You can copy and paste the preceding command from http://bit.ly/1F3TmdJ.

In either case, you should see output similar to the following:

```
bigfoot:hipstr ryanbaldwin$ find . -print | sed -e 's;[^/]*/;|____;g;s;____|; |;g'
.
|____.gitignore
|____Procfile
|____project.clj
|____README.md
|____resources
| |____public
| | |____css
| | | |____screen.css
| | |____fonts
| | | |____glyphicons-halflings-regular.eot
| | | |____glyphicons-halflings-regular.svg
| | | |____glyphicons-halflings-regular.ttf
| | | |____glyphicons-halflings-regular.woff
| | |____img
| | |____js
| | |____md
| | | |____docs.md
| |____templates
| | |____about.html
| | |____base.html
| | |____home.html
|____src
| |____hipstr
| | |____handler.clj
| | |____layout.clj
| | |____middleware.clj
| | |____repl.clj
| | |____routes
| | | |____home.clj
| | |____session_manager.clj
| | |____util.clj
|____test
| |____hipstr
| | |____test
| | | |____handler.clj
bigfoot:hipstr ryanbaldwin$      cd ..
```

Luminus generates three directories at the root of the application directory: resources, src, and test.

The resources directory contains the files that will compose the front end of our applications. The public folder contains resources publicly available to the client, such as our JavaScript, CSS, and images. By contrast, the templates directory contains our Selmer templates used for the heavy rendering of HTML parts. All of these files will be made available on our class path; however, only those in the public folder will be actually available to the client.

The `src` directory contains all of the necessary namespaces for running our application, and the `test` directory contains all the necessary namespaces for testing our `src`.

In addition to the directories, however, Luminus also generated some files in the `src` directory. These files are the bare minimum requirement to successfully run our application, and each one handles specific functionality. Let's take a brief look at the base functionality contained in each file.

# util.clj

The `hipstr.util` namespace is a simple namespace where you can put various helper functions you find yourself frequently using during the development of your application. Out of the box, Luminus generates a `hipstr.util` namespace with a single function, `md->html`, which converts markdown into HTML. Typically, I try to avoid namespaces such as `util.clj` because they eventually turn into the junk drawer in your kitchen, but they can be useful on smaller projects if things don't get too crowded. The following block of code shows the `hipstr.util` namespace:

```
(ns hipstr.util
  (:require [noir.io :as io]
            [markdown.core :as md]))

(defn md->html
  "reads a markdown file from public/md and returns an HTML
   string"
  [filename]
  (md/md-to-html-string (io/slurp-resource filename)))
```

# session_manager.clj

One of lib-noir's exposed functionalities is session management (which we'll discuss in detail in *Chapter 10, Sessions and Cookies*). The default session pool in Luminus is an *in-memory* session pool, a shortcoming of which is that expired sessions are only removed from memory when the server handles a request associated with an expired session. As a result, old stale sessions can linger in memory indefinitely, straining memory resources on the server. Luminus boilerplates a `cronj` job in the `hipstr.sessions-manager` namespace, which occasionally removes stale, unused sessions. By default, the job runs every 30 minutes. Take a look at the following lines of code:

```
(ns hipstr.session-manager
  (:require [noir.session :refer [clear-expired-sessions]]
            [cronj.core :refer [cronj]]))
```

```
(def cleanup-job
  (cronj
    :entries
    [{:id "session-cleanup"
      :handler (fn [_ _] (clear-expired-sessions))
      :schedule "* /30 * * * *"
      :opts {}}]))
```

# layout.clj

The `hipstr.layout` namespace houses the functions that are used to render the HTTP response body. By default, Luminus creates a single function, `render`, which will render any Selmer template onto the HTTP response.The following lines of code is for the `hipstr.layout` namespace:

```
(ns hipstr.layout
  (:require [selmer.parser :as parser]
            [clojure.string :as s]
            [ring.util.response :refer [content-type response]]
            [compojure.response :refer [Renderable]]
            [environ.core :refer [env]]))

(def template-path "templates/")

(deftype RenderableTemplate [template params]
  Renderable
  (render [this request]
    (content-type
      (->> (assoc params
        (keyword
        (s/replace template #".html" "-selected"))"active"
          :dev (env :dev)
            :servlet-context
              (if-let [context (:servlet-context request)]
              ;; If we're not inside a serlvet environment
              ;; (for example when using mock requests), then
              ;; .getContextPath might not exist
              (try (.getContextPath context)
                (catch IllegalArgumentException _

                context))))
            (parser/render-file (str template-path template))
          response)
```

```
                    "text/html; charset=utf-8")))

(defn render [template & [params]]
(RenderableTemplate. template params))
```

The key to the `hipstr.layout` namespace is that it remains high level and generic. You should avoid writing functions with domain knowledge in this namespace, and instead focus on generating response bodies. If you put an explicit URL or filename in this namespace, you're probably doing it wrong.

# middleware.clj

Middleware, for the unfamiliar, is a function that can work with an incoming request prior to the request being handled by the main application (that is our proverbial *business logic*). Its function is similar to how a car moves through an assembly line; each employee working the line is responsible for interacting with the car in some specific way. Much like how at the end of the assembly line the car is in its final state and ready for consumption, so is the request in its final state and ready for processing by the main application. The following code is for the `hipstr.middleware` namespace:

```
(ns hipstr.middleware
  (:require [taoensso.timbre :as timbre]
            [selmer.parser :as parser]
            [environ.core :refer [env]]
            [selmer.middleware :refer [wrap-error-page]]
            [prone.middleware :refer [wrap-exceptions]]
            [noir-exception.core :refer [wrap-internal-error]]))

(defn log-request [handler]
  (fn [req]
    (timbre/debug req)
    (handler req)))

(def development-middleware
  [wrap-error-page
   wrap-exceptions])

(def production-middleware
  [#(wrap-internal-error % :log (fn [e] (timbre/error e)))])

(defn load-middleware []
  (concat (when (env :dev) development-middleware)
          production-middleware))
```

The `hipstr.middleware` namespace has two primary responsibilities. The first is that it ties together all the different middleware we want across any of our runtime environments. The second is that it gives us a place to add additional middleware, if desired. Of course, there's nothing prohibiting us from writing our middleware in a new namespace, but for the sake of simplicity and for this book, we'll simply create additional middleware in the `hipstr.middleware` namespace.

# routes/home.clj

One of the directories that Luminus generated was a route folder. Routes are what tie a request to a specific handler (or, in layman's terms, a chunk of code to be executed based on the URL the request is sent to). Luminus generates 2 routes for us:

- A / route, which renders the result of calling the `home-page` function, which ultimately renders the home page you see at startup
- A /about route, which renders the result of the `about-page` function, responsible for rendering the `about.html` page

Take a look at the following lines of code:

```
(ns hipstr.routes.home
  (:require [compojure.core :refer :all]
            [hipstr.layout :as layout]
            [hipstr.util :as util]))

(defn home-page []
  (layout/render
    "home.html" {:content (util/md->html "/md/docs.md")}))

(defn about-page []
  (layout/render "about.html"))

(defroutes home-routes
  (GET "/" [] (home-page))
  (GET "/about" [] (about-page)))
```

We will create a couple of our own routing namespaces over the course of this book. The routes we'll create in those namespaces will follow the same pattern demonstrated in the preceding `hipster.routes.home` namespace. We'll talk a bit more about routes in *Chapter 4, URL Routing and Template Rendering*.

# handler.clj

Everything we've seen in this chapter is brought together into a single, harmonious, running application in the hipstr.handler namespace, explained in the following lines of code. Opening the file for a cursory scan reveals our cron job to clean up expired sessions, the home-routes from the hipstr.routes.home namespace, the configuration of our Timbre logging, and so on.

```clojure
(ns hipstr.handler
  (:require [compojure.core :refer [defroutes]]
    ; ... snipped for brevity …
    [cronj.core :as cronj]))

(defroutes base-routes
  (route/resources "/")
  (route/not-found "Not Found"))

(defn init
  "init will be called once when
    app is deployed as a servlet on
    an app server such as Tomcat
    put any initialization code here"
  []
  ;… snipped for brevity …)

(defn destroy
  "destroy will be called when your application
   shuts down, put any clean up code here"
  []
  ; ... snipped for brevity ...)

;; timeout sessions after 30 minutes
(def session-defaults
  {:timeout (* 60 30)
   :timeout-response (redirect "/")})

(defn- mk-defaults
      "set to true to enable XSS protection"
      [xss-protection?]
      ;... snipped for brevity ...
)

(def app (app-handler
          ;; add your application routes here
```

```
      [home-routes base-routes]
      ;; add custom middleware here
      :middleware (load-middleware)
      :ring-defaults (mk-defaults false)
      ;; add access rules here
      :access-rules []
      ;; serialize/deserialize the following data formats
      ;; available formats:
      ;; :json :json-kw :yaml :yaml-kw :edn :yaml-in-html
      :formats [:json-kw :edn :transit-json]))
```

We'll get into detail about what all is happening, and when, in *Chapter 2, Ring and the Ring Server.*

# repl.clj

The last Luminus generated namespace, hipstr.repl, is one that often confuses beginners because it's strikingly similar to hipster.handler. The hipstr.repl namespace has a start-server and stop-server function, much like hipster. handler. However, hipstr.repl allows us to start and stop our development server from the Clojure REPL. This might seem like a weird thing to do, but by running our server from the REPL we can modify our running system and the changes will be "automagically" reloaded in our server. No need for the time consuming and frustrating "compile-deploy-restart-grab-a-coffee-and-twiddle-your-thumbs cycle!"

```
(ns hipstr.repl
  (:use hipstr.handler
        ring.server.standalone
        [ring.middleware file-info file]))

(defonce server (atom nil))

(defn get-handler []
  ;; #'app expands to (var app) so that when we reload our code,
  ;; the server is forced to re-resolve the symbol in the var
  ;; rather than having its own copy. When the root binding
  ;; changes, the server picks it up without having to restart.
  ; ... snipped for brevity ...
)

(defn start-server
  "used for starting the server in development mode from REPL"
  [& [port]]
```

```
    ; ... snipped for brevity ...
  )

(defn stop-server []
  ;… snipped for brevity …
  )
```

Incorporating the REPL into your development workflow is a wonderful thing to do. You can load your namespace into the REPL while you work on it and test the code while you're developing right then and there. In fact, some IDEs such as **LightTable** take this a step further, and will "live-evaluate" your code as you type. The ability of running the `dev` server from the REPL completes the circle.

 If you're not currently using a decent IDE for Clojure development, I strongly encourage you to give LightTable a try. It's free, open source, lightweight, and very different than anything you're used to. It's quite good. Check it out at `http://www.lighttable.com`.

# Summary

In this chapter, you learned how to generate a new Clojure-based web application using Leiningen and the Luminus template. We also got a high-level understanding of each dependency, and how Luminus structures its projects. In the next chapter we'll take a detailed look at the Ring and Ring Server libraries, and what they're responsible for. It sounds a little dry, I know, but I recommend that you read it. There will be cake and punch at the end, but without all the calories of cake and punch.

# 2
# Ring and the Ring Server

In the last chapter, we generated a new web application using the Luminus template. However, before we get too deep into the development of our app and playing with all the toys, it's important for us to get a high-level understanding of two technologies that will support everything we build and do, and that's Ring and the Ring Server.

## Understanding Ring in Clojure

> *"Ring is a Clojure web applications library inspired by Python's WSGI and Ruby's Rack. By abstracting the details of HTTP into a simple, unified API, Ring allows web applications to be constructed of modular components that can be shared among a variety of applications, web servers, and web frameworks."*

> *- James Reeves*

James Reeves is also known as Weavejester; he is the creator and maintainer of Ring and about a billion other Clojure-based technologies (`https://github.com/ring-clojure/ring/blob/master/README.md`).

In simple terms, Ring handles all the nitty gritty HTTP implementation details, such as HTTP request/response, parameters, cookies, and so on. It abstracts the underlying implementations away from our code, allowing us to focus on writing our application instead of low-level HTTP crud. This abstraction, coupled with the fact that Ring is built on top of the HTTP Servlet specification, enables us to package our application and host it in a variety of servlet containers, such as GlassFish (`https://glassfish.java.net`), Tomcat (`http://tomcat.apache.org`), and Jetty (`http://eclipse.org/jetty`).

We can even run our application as a standalone, which is actually the easiest and most popular way of running a web application written in Clojure and using Ring. This is made possible thanks to the embedded Jetty server, which if we wanted could also be swapped out for **http-kit** (http://http-kit.org), a highly efficient HTTP client/server for Clojure.

At a high level, Ring is composed of 5 components: **request maps**, **response maps**, **handlers**, **middleware**, and **adapters**.

# Request maps

Ring represents HTTP requests as simple Clojure maps, whose keys are drawn from the Java Servlet API and the official documentation *RFC2616 – Hypertext Transfer Protocol - HTTP/1.1* (http://www.w3.org/Protocols/rfc2616/rfc2616.html). Practically speaking, the request map contains the following keys:

- :server-port: This is the port on which the request is being handled.

- :server-name: This is the resolved name or IP address of the server handling the request.

- :remote-addr: This is the IP address of the client, which is making the request.

- :uri: This is the part of the address after the domain name. For example, for the address http://ryans.io/some/beautiful/uri, the request map's :uri would be /some/beautiful/uri.

- :query-string: This is the HTTP query string of the request, if one exists. For example, for the address http://ryans.io/some/beautiful/uri?color=blue&favPrime=7, the request map's :query-string would be color=blue&favPrime=7.

- :scheme: This is the protocol used to make the request as a keyword; :http for HTTP request, and :https for Secure HTTP.

- :request-method: This is the HTTP method used to make the request as a keyword, so it will be one of :get, :post, :put, :delete, :head, or :options keys.

- :headers: This is a map of the header names (as lowercased string) to header values (also as string). Here's a sample code:

```
{:headers {"content-type" "text/html"
  "content-length" "500"
  "pragma" "no-cache"}}
```

- :body: This is a string of any contents in the request body itself (such as the contents of an HTTP POST request).

The request maps, however, are not restricted to this information, and often contain additional keys. Middleware, as we'll see later, can mutate the request map by adding additional keys.

# Response maps

Similar to request maps, Ring represents an HTTP response as a simple Clojure map. The response map contains only three keys:

- `:status`: This is the HTTP status code of the response as an integer, such as `200` or `403`. A full list of HTTP status codes is made available as part of the RFC2616, and can be viewed at `http://www.w3.org/Protocols/rfc2616/rfc2616-sec10.html`. I urge you to take a read—it's surprisingly interesting!

- `:headers`: Similar to the one of request map, `:headers` contains a map of header names (string) to header values.

- `:body`: This is the body of the response. This can be one of the following four types, and the behavior will change for each:
  - When a `String`, the body is sent directly to the client as is
  - When an `ISeq`, each element of the sequence is sent to the client as a `String`
  - When a `File`, the contents of the file will be sent to the client
  - When an `InputStream`, the contents of the stream are sent to the client, after which the stream is closed

An example of a simple `Hello World!` response map can look like this:

```
{:status 200
 :headers {"Content-Type" "text/html"}
 :body "<html><body><h1>Hello, World!</h1></body></html>"}
```

# Handlers

A **handler** is a Clojure function that accepts a request map and returns a response map, that is, *process the incoming request* and *return a response*. Here's an example code:

```
(defn hello-world
  "Simply produces a Hello World Response Map for some mythical,
    useless application."
  [request]
  {:status 200
    :headers {"Content-Type" "text/html"}
    :body "<html><body><h1>Hello, World!</h1></body></html>"})
```

Handlers are the core of our application. Typically our URLs will map one-to-one with a handler.

Let's create our own handler, and remap one of our routes to use it instead of the default Luminus generated one. Don't fret if this doesn't make complete sense to you right now — it will within a couple of chapters. Perform the following steps (assume that all paths are from the root of the Luminus-generated hipstr application):

1. Open the `src/hipstr/routes/home.clj` file.

2. Above the call to `defroutes`, add the following handler:

```
(defn foo-response []
  {:status 200
    :headers {"Content-Type" "text/html"}
    :body "<html><body><h1>Hello World!</h1></body>
  </html>"})
```

3. Modify the `/about` route (the last line in the file) to use the `foo-response` handler instead of the `home-page` handler:

```
(GET "/about" [] (foo-response))
```

4. Open your browser and navigate to `http://localhost:3000/about`. You'll now see a simple **Hello World!** instead of the default Luminus About page:

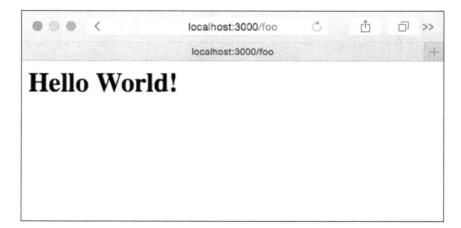

> Remember to keep your server running while reading this book, as we'll be doing boatloads of examples. Boatloads! You can start the development server by executing the following command from the root of your hipstr source directory:
>
> `# lein ring server`

Congrats! You just wrote your first handler! Pretty simple, right? Don't worry if this didn't make a whole lot of sense, we'll go into more detail in *Chapter 4, URL Routing and Template Rendering*.

# Middleware

Middleware, as described in *Chapter 1, Getting Started With Luminus*, are functions that sit between the adapter and the handler. A middleware function accepts a handler and returns a new handler function. Middleware functions have complete access to the request map and/or response map. As such, middleware functions can perform some type of action on the map (such as adding a key, or logging the map to file) before passing it on to the handler.

As an example, let's write a middleware function that adds a completely meaningless yet excitable key to the request map, `:go-bowling?`, and then consume this key in the handler we just created:

1.  Open the `src/hisptr/middleware.clj` file.

2.  Right after the namespace declaration, add the following function, which takes a handler, and returns a new handler function (which in turn adds a new key to the request map and calls the next handler in the chain):

    ```
    (defn go-bowling? [handler]
      (fn [request]
        (let [request (assoc request :go-bowling? "YES! NOW!")]
          (handler request))))
    ```

3.  In the `development-middleware` definition, add our new go-bowling middleware:

    ```
    (def development-middleware
      [go-bowling?
       wrap-error-page
       wrap-exceptions])
    ```

4.  Back in the `src/hipstr/routes/home.clj`, adjust the `:body` value in our foo-response handler to emit the `:go-bowling?` key on the request map. Don't forget to adjust the handler's parameters to accept the request map:

    ```
    (defn foo-response [request]
      {:status 200
       :headers {"Content-Type" "text/html"}
       :body (str "<html><body><dt>Go bowling?</dt>"
       "<dd>"(:go-bowling? request)"</dd></body></
    html>")})
    ```

5.  Lastly, change the `/about` route to make use of the request map:

    ```
    (GET "/about" request (foo-response request))
    ```

6.  Finally, refresh your page at `http://localhost:3000/about` and see our middleware in action!

You just became a middleware wizard! If you'd like more information about middleware and how it's natively used in Ring, check out `https://github.com/ring-clojure/ring/wiki/Concepts#middleware`.

# Adapters

Adapters are the glue between the underlying HTTP and our handlers. The Ring library comes with a Jetty adapter (`[ring/ring-jetty-adapter "1.3.0"]`), which sits between a Jetty servlet container and the rest of the application stack. At a high level, an adapter will convert the incoming HTTP request into a request map, pass the map off to a handler, and then convert the returned response map into the appropriate servlet HTTP response to send back to the client.

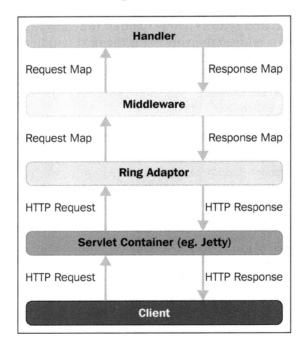

Knowing how to write adapters is beyond the scope of this book, and is something you do not need to know in order to build a web application using Clojure.

# What is the Ring Server?

The first thing to know is that Ring and the Ring Server are not, I repeat, are not the same thing. Whereas Ring provides a suite of libraries which abstract the underlying implementation details, the Ring Server library provides the ability to start an actual web server to serve a Ring handler.

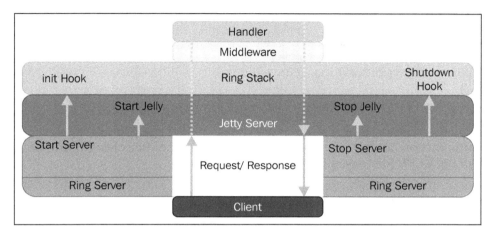

Whenever we use `lein ring server` from the command line, we start the Ring Server (there are other ways, but we'll get to those later in this chapter, and in *Chapter 11, Environment Configuration and Deployment*). At startup, the Ring Server will execute any registered application *initialization hooks*, and then start an embedded Jetty server, which serves our *application handler*. Incoming requests are then processed by Ring, as described in the previous section, until we shut down our app. On shutdown, Ring stops the embedded Jetty server and executes any registered shutdown hooks.

We can see this in the interaction between our `hipstr.handler` and `hipstr.repl` namespaces. Let's examine the `hipstr.handler` namespace, and then we'll see how the `hipstr.repl` namespace uses it.

## hipstr.handler

The `hipstr.handler` namespace is the bootstrap to our application. In this, we define an initialization hook, a shutdown hook, a couple of application routes, and the application handler.

# Initialization hooks

The `hipstr.handler/init` defines the initialization hook to be invoke immediately before starting the embedded Jetty server. Typically, we add any kind of application runtime configuration and invoke any other components required for the duration of the application. For example, our application configures various Timbre logging appenders and initiates the session manager.

```
(defn init
  "init will be called once when app is deployed as a servlet on
  an app server such as Tomcat
  put any initialization code here"
  []
  ;…snipped for brevity…
)
```

This initialization hook is configured for use either in the project configuration or through the REPL (discussed later).

# Shutdown hooks

The `hipstr.handler/destroy` defines the shutdown hook to invoke immediately before exiting. The application shutdown hook is a function that performs anything our application needs to do before it permanently exits, such as stopping the session manager, or emitting a log statement stating the application is shutting down:

```
(defn destroy
  "destroy will be called when your application
  shuts down, put any clean up code here"
  []
  ;…snipped for brevity…)
```

The shutdown hook is configured for use either in the project configuration, or through the REPL (again, which we'll discuss shortly).

# App routes

Routes are what tie a request to a specific Ring handler, that is, which URL should execute which chunk of code. The Compojure library provides us the tools to tie these two things together. We've already played with these earlier in the chapter, when we fooled around with the /About route to execute the `foo-response` handler.

The `hipstr.handler/app-routes` defines two special `defroutes`: `route/resources` and `route/not-found`.

```
(defroutes app-routes
  (route/resources "/")
  (route/not-found "Not Found"))
```

The `(route/resources "/")` route defines the URL from which our static resources will be served (found in the `hipstr/resources/public directory`). For example, the URL to our `hipstr/resources/public/css/screen.css` file would simply be `/css/screen.css`. If we changed our resources route to `(route/resources "/artifacts/")`, then the URL to the same `screen.css` file would be `/artifacts/css/screen.css`.

The `(route/not-found "Not Found")` defines what should be emitted for a `404 Not Found` HTTP response. The `luminus` template simply defaults to `Not Found` (in practice, you'll likely want to have a handler that renders something a little more pretty). Ring will take the `"Not Found"` parameter and insert it into the `<body>` element of an HTML document on our behalf.

 True story: Ring puts anything that isn't a Clojure map inside the `<body>` element, whereas a map will be treated as a Ring response.

# The application handler

The real meat of the `hipstr.handler` namespace is the application handler. This is where we package together the various routes and middleware, define how we want our sessions to behave, any access rules to protected routes (for example, authenticated-only pages), and which formats should be serialized/deserialized to /from EDN in the requests/responses. Let's define the application handler:

```
(def app (app-handler
  ;; add your application routes here
  [home-routes app-routes]
  ;; add custom middleware here
  :middleware (load-middleware)
  ;; timeout sessions after 30 minutes
  :session-options {:timeout (* 60 30)
  :timeout-response (redirect "/")}
  ;; add access rules here
  :access-rules []
```

```
;; serialize/deserialize the following data formats
;; available formats:
;; :json :json-kw :yaml :yaml-kw :edn :yaml-in-html
:formats [:json-kw :edn]))
```

The app handler packages our entire application, which will receive the request maps from Ring, and return response maps. As we build on our hipstr example, we will be modifying this function to include our own routes, access rules, and so on.

# hipstr.repl

The hipstr.handler namespace defines what and how our application works, whereas the hipstr.repl namespace actually consumes it and makes it all run through the Clojure REPL. The hipstr.repl namespace is considerably more simple than the hipstr.handler namespace; it merely consists of an atom (to store a Jetty server instance returned from the Ring Server library), a start-server function, a stop-server function, and a get-handler function.

## Start-server

The hipstr.repl/start-server function attempts to start the Ring Server on a given port, defaulting to port 3000. It also forwards the application handler (returned from get-handler) along with any runtime options, to the underlying Jetty server (a full list of which is defined at https://github.com/weavejester/ring-server#usage). Here is the code for starting the Ring Server:

```
;... Snipped for brevity
(defonce server (atom nil))
;...

(defn start-server
  "used for starting the server in development mode from REPL"
  [& [port]]
  (let [port (if port (Integer/parseInt port) 3000)]
    (reset! server
      (serve (get-handler)
        {:port port
        :init init                              ;#1
        :auto-reload? true
        :destroy destroy                        ;#2
        :join? false}))                         ;#3
        (println (str "You can view the site at http://localhost:"
port)))))
```

The :init and :destroy keys at #1 and #2 configure the initialization and shutdown hooks, respectively. The :join? option at #3 will determine if the thread will wait until the underlying Jetty instance stops. When set to false, the Ring Server will return the actual Jetty instance, which we keep a reference to in the server atom. When running the server through the REPL, it's best to keep this option set to false, thereby allowing us to stop the server without having to kill our REPL session.

# Stop-server

The stop-server function simply stops the retained Jetty instance, and then destroys it.

```
(defn stop-server []
  (.stop @server)
  (reset! server nil))
```

The server is now magically stopped.

# Get-handler

The get-handler function returns our hipstr.handler/app handler, exposes the static resources directory, and wraps the handler with one last bit of middleware, which adds a couple more headers to the response. The added middleware also returns a 304 Not Modified response if it detects the document being served hasn't been modified since the previous request:

```
(defn get-handler []
  ;; #'app expands to (var app) so that when we reload our code,
  ;; the server is forced to re-resolve the symbol in the var
  ;; rather than having its own copy. When the root binding
  ;; changes, the server picks it up without having to restart.
  (-> #'app
    ; Makes static assets in
    ; $PROJECT_DIR/resources/public/ available.
    (wrap-file "resources")
    ; Content-Type, Content-Length, and Last Modified headers
    ; for files in body
    (wrap-file-info)))
```

# Configuring and running the Ring Server

There are two ways you can run the Ring Server. The first is by loading the `hipstr.repl` namespace into a REPL and calling `start-server`. The second is from the command line (which we've seen earlier):

```
# lein ring server
```

In either case, an embedded Jetty server will be spun up to serve our application handler, and a browser will pop open. If you don't want the browser to open, you can run the server in the `headless` mode:

```
# lein ring server-headless
```

How we start the server determines how we configure the server. We've already seen how to configure the server when running through the REPL (by adjusting the options map that's passed as part of the call to `ring.server.standalone/serve`), but how do we configure the server if running from the command line?

The `lein ring` command is made available through the `lein-ring` plugin. Luminus includes this plugin when generating the project for us. In our project dependencies file (`project.clj`), you'll see the following lines of code:

```
:plugins [[lein-ring "0.8.13"]
[lein-environ "1.0.0"]
[lein-ancient "0.5.5"]]
```

The plugin offers a few useful subtasks, but the immediately beneficial ones are the `server` and `server-headless` subtasks.

Both of these subtasks will use the same configuration, configured in our project.clj, immediately following the plugins section:

```
:ring {:handler hipstr.handler/app
  :init    hipstr.handler/init
  :destroy hipstr.handler/destroy}
```

The options map should look familiar, as it's nearly identical to the options map we pass into the call to `ring.server.standalone/serve` in the `hipstr.repl` namespace. The main difference is the `:handler` option, which points to our `hipstr.handler/app` application handler, whereas in the `hipstr.repl` namespace we pass the handler directly. In essence, running the Ring Server from the command line does what we do in `hipstr.repl/start-server`.

You can play around starting the Ring Server from the command line and specifying some additional options as defined at `https://github.com/weavejester/ring-server#usage`. For example, try setting the `:open-browser?` option to `false`.

```
:ring {:handler hipstr.handler/app
  :init hipstr.handler/init
  :destroy  hipstr.handler/destroy
  :open-browser? false}
```

With `:open-browser?` set to `false` our `lein ring server` will no longer open a browser, much like `lein ring server-headless`.

# Summary

Congratulations on successfully making it through the driest chapter in the book! A cruel but necessary exercise. In this chapter, you learned the difference between Ring and the Ring Server. We got a taste of how to modify route behavior by creating a new route handler, and played around with a bit of middleware. Finally, you learned how to start and stop the Ring Server from both the REPL and the command line, and how to configure each, respectively. In the next chapter, we're going to take a look at a developer's best and only set of binoculars—logging.

# 3
# Logging

We've read patiently and slugged our way through *Chapter 2*, *Ring and the Ring Server*, learning the technicalities about request and response maps, handlers, middleware, and adapters. The time has come for us to start getting our hands dirty.

Logging is a wonderful tool in development, and is essential for successfully debugging a system that's gone completely haywire. Logging is the eyes, ears, and mouth of our system. It is our saving grace. However, logging traditionally has a dark side. If you've ever used Java or .NET, you'll be well versed in log4j and log4net, and all the excruciatingly painful configurations that go along with it. While logging is extremely useful, setting it up correctly is nothing short of a clinic in patience.

In this chapter, you will learn:

- How to configure Timbre for logging
- How to reconfigure one of the appenders configured by Luminus
- How to configure a new appender from scratch
- How to emit logging statements

## What is Timbre?

Timbre is a full Clojure library for logging. It's fast, has low overhead, and has many interesting appenders out of the box. Most importantly, setting it up is relatively easy and straightforward compared to other logging libraries.

# What is an appender?

An **appender** is the term used for anything that emits a logging statement to a destination. For example, a logger that writes logging statements to a file is referred to as a file appender, and a logger that writes to a MongoDB database is a MongoDB appender (which natively exists in Timbre). Basically, appender is a fancy pants term for "writer". In the world of Timbre, an appender is, technically, just a map of options, one of which is the appender function responsible for performing the actual logging.

# Configuring a Timbre appender

An appender's configuration is managed by a single function, `timbre/set-config!`, which accepts a list of keys identifying the type of appender, and the appender map, which is the actual configuration for the appender.

Taking a look at the `init` function in `hipstr.handler`, the first thing we see is a call to configure Timbre:

```
(timbre/set-config!
  [:appenders :rotor]
  {:min-level :info
    :enabled? true
    :async? false ; should be always false for rotor
    :max-message-per-msecs nil
    :fn rotor/appender-fn})
```

The preceding snippet configures the rotor appender, a type of file appender that creates a new log file after the current log file exceeds a specific size. Timbre's `set-config!` has a similar signature and behavior to Clojure's `assoc-in` (https://clojuredocs.org/clojure.core/assoc-in) function, but without having to define the target map to mutate.

> To see all the different appenders that Timbre ships with and to see how to configure each of them, take a look at the appenders' source at https://github.com/ptaoussanis/timbre/tree/master/src/taoensso/timbre/appenders.

# Timbre log levels

A log level is the severity of a log message. In order, from lowest to highest, the seven Timbre log levels are :trace, :debug, :info, :warn, :error, :fatal, and :report. We can configure which appenders listen to which log levels by either setting a global log level using Timbre's set-level!, or on a case-by-case basis when configuring an appender using :min-level, as we did in our preceding example snippet.

> There are other ways to set global or thread-level minimum log levels, but they're not as convenient or useful. You can read more about those in the configuration section of the Timbre documentation. To see all the different appenders that Timbre ships with, take a look at the appenders' source at https://github.com/ptaoussanis/timbre/tree/master/src/taoensso/timbre/appenders.

We can configure multiple appenders with multiple calls to set-config!, and each appender can respond to a different minimum logging level. For example, perhaps you'll want to use a file appender for the :info level and above, but for anything fatal, you'll want to also use an email appender (also included as part of the Timbre library, called a postal appender). This can be done by either explicitly setting :min-level on each appender's configuration, or by setting the global minimum log level to be :info using Timbre's set-level! setting and overriding it on any appender that requires a different minimum level. Take a look at the following code sample:

```
(require '[taoensso.timbre :as timbre]
         '[taoensso.timbre.appenders.postal :as postal])
(timbre/set-level! :info)
(timbre/set-config! [:appenders :postal]
        (postal/make-postal-appender
          {:minlevel :fatal}
          ;...snipped for brevity...
        ))
```

In the preceding snippet, we set a global minimum log level of :info using set-level!. However, we override the global level in our :postal appender such that the appender only fires off emails for any log statements that are at least :fatal.

# Appender configuration keys

As `timbre/set-config!` is modeled after Clojure's `assoc-in` call, the keys we pass must map to Timbre's internal, nested configuration map. The appender's configuration keys typically match the name of the appender's namespace, so the configuration of the `taoensso.timbre.appenders.rotor` key is `[:appenders :rotor]`, the configuration of the `taoensso.timbre.appenders.mongo` key is `[:appenders :mongo]`, and so on. However, it's always best to take a quick peek at the code on GitHub to ensure that you're using the correct keys.

# Appender map

The appender map, like the appender configuration keys, is specific to the appender you're configuring. Each appender will have its own set of options defining it how it should behave (such as `:path` for the rotor appender). However, there is a set of configuration keys that are common to all appenders:

- `:min-level`: This is an optional key and the minimum emitted log level required to actually append to the target. By default it is set to all levels.

- `:enabled?`: This is an optional key and it has a `true`/`false` value, which enables/disables the appender. By default it is set to `false`.

- `:async?`: This is an optional key and it also has a `true`/`false` value, which when true, will call the appender asynchronously (good for slower appenders, such as a database appender or a socket appender). By default it is set to `false`.

- `:rate-limit`: This is an optional key and limits the number of appender calls per millisecond. By default it is set to no limit.

- `:fn`: This is a required key and the function for the appender in question.

There are a few other more advanced options but you'll rarely, if ever, need to use them. You can read the full list of available appender configuration options at `https://github.com/ptaoussanis/timbre#configuration`.

# Shared appender configuration

The next thing we notice in the `hipstr.handler` namespace, after the configuration of the rotor appender, is the shared configuration.

```
(timbre/set-config!
  [:shared-appender-config :rotor]
  {:path "hipstr.log" :max-size (* 512 1024) :backlog 10})
```

The :shared-appender-config is a configuration shared across all appenders, despite each appender having its own section within the shared configuration. It's *shared* in the sense that it's blindly sent to each appender at runtime, and each appender knows which section to interrogate to get its settings. It's like having a shared cheese plate that you pass around to dinner guests, but each piece of cheese is different and is labeled with a specific guest's name. It's that kind of "share".

The rotor appender uses [:shared-appender-config :rotor] for some of its values. We know this by checking the docstring in the taoensso.timbre. appenders.rotor namespace, as follows:

```
(def rotor-appender
  {:doc (str "Simple Rotating File Appender.\n"
             "Needs :rotor config map in :shared-appender-config,
e.g.:
             {:path \"logs/app.log\"
              :max-size (* 512 1024)
              :backlog 5}")
```

You will often need to add an additional configuration to :shared-appender-config for the appender you want to use. This is one of those weird idiosyncratic "*gotchas!*" that often appear when it comes to logging.

# Logging with Timbre

We can emit a log statement using Timbre's log function, which accepts — at a minimum — the log level and a message to emit. The following code shows an example of an log function.

```
(require '[taoensso.timbre :as timbre])
(timbre/log :info "This is an info message.")
>> 2014-Nov-24 14:35:24 -0500 computer.local INFO [hipstr.handler] -
This is an info message.
```

Alternatively, Timbre makes available a function for each logging level, thus relieving us from having to specify the log level with each call, as shown in the following code:

```
(timbre/info "This is an info message.")
```

Timbre's log functions are similar to Clojure's str and println functions, as we can pass multiple strings to produce a single long string:

```
(timbre/info "This" "is" "an" "info" "message.")
```

No logging framework would be complete without the ability to log exceptions. Here is an example of appending an Exception:

```
(timbre/error (Exception. "Aw snap!") "Something bad happened." "It's
really awful.")
```

Appenders will only emit messages that are emitted at a log level equal or higher to their minimum log level. As such, the following will not actually emit anything.

```
(timbre/set-level! :warn)
(timbre/debug "You will never see this.")
```

As `:debug` is a lower log level than `:warn`, the preceding debug message will not be emitted.

# Adding an appender

Luminus generates our application to use the rotor appender. I prefer using a rolling appender instead of a rotor appender. A rolling appender is a file appender, like the rotor appender, however, it doesn't create a new log file when a predetermined maximum size is hit. Instead, a new log file is created either daily, weekly, or monthly. I find rolling appenders more useful in production environments because they help when diagnosing problems that have happened sometime in the past (you have a better idea which log files to check).

In this section, we're going to configure a rolling appender for our hipstr application.

# Adding the rolling appender

We can put our rolling logs in their own directory, called `logs`. Unfortunately, Timbre doesn't create directories for us, so we'll have to create the directory first. From the terminal, add a `logs` directory in the hipstr source root:

```
# mkdir logs
```

Next, in our `hipstr.handler` namespace, we'll want to refer to the `taoensso.timbre.appenders.rolling` namespace. In the `:require` block, add the following lines of code below the rotor import:

```
(:require ;...snipped for brevity...
  [taoensso.timbre.appenders.rotor :as rotor]
  [taoensso.timbre.appenders.rolling :as rolling]
  ...)
```

To add a rolling appender, we will use the assistance of the `rolling/make-rolling-appender` function, which returns a rolling appender map with some defaults set (`:enabled? true, :min-level nil, :pattern :daily`). However, we can also override these defaults by passing in an override map when we make the call, as shown in the following code snippet. Add the following block of code to the start of the `hipstr.handler/init` function:

```
(timbre/set-config!
 [:appenders :rolling]
 (rolling/make-rolling-appender {:min-level :info}))
```

Next, configure the location where the log files should be emitted. We specify this in the same place as we did for the rotor appender, as part of `:shared-appender-config` using following lines of code:

```
(timbre/set-config!
 [:shared-appender-config :rolling :path] "logs/hipstr.log")
```

Finally, we remove the two calls to `timbre/set-config!` that deal with the rotor appender, thus removing any logging to the original `hipstr.log` file in the hipstr root. The final logging configuration in `hipstr.handler/init` is now simply this:

```
(timbre/set-config!
 [:appenders :rolling]
 (rolling/make-rolling-appender {:min-level :info}))

(timbre/set-config!
 [:shared-appender-config :rolling :path] "logs/hipstr.log")
```

With the preceding logging configurations intact, any log statements with a log level of `:info` or above will be logged to the `logs/hipstr.log` file. In addition, the `logs/hipstr.log` file will always be the current day's log file, and log files from previous days will be found in the `logs` directory with the pattern `hipstr.log.[year][month][day]`.

# Summary

It is always confounding to configure logging libraries. In this chapter, you learned that it doesn't have to be impossible when using Timbre. You learned how to configure existing appenders, as well as adding new ones, and you learned the value of always reading the friendly manual… even if the manual is docstrings in the source code. You can use your new found knowledge and love for Timbre if you need to debug anything in the next chapter, wherein we will discuss Compojure route handlers, Selmer templates, and we'll finally create our first page.

# 4
# URL Routing and Template Rendering

So far, we've looked at the basics of getting our codebase into a state where we can start developing some of the meat of our application. It hasn't been very exciting, I know. In this chapter, however, we will start building our application, creating actual endpoints that process HTTP requests, which return something we can look at. In this chapter, we will:

- Learn what the Compojure routing library is and how it works
- Build our own Compojure routes to handle an incoming request
- Learn what the Selmer rendering library is and how it works
- Create our own Selmer HTML template

 What this chapter won't cover, however, is making any of our HTML pretty, client-side frameworks, or JavaScript. Our goal is to understand the server-side/Clojure components and get up and running as quickly as possible. As a result, our templates are going to look pretty basic, if not downright embarrassing.

## What is Compojure?

Compojure is a small, simple library that allows us to create specific request handlers for specific URLs and HTTP methods. In other words, "HTTP Method *A* requesting URL *B* will execute Clojure function *C*". By allowing us to do this, we can create our application in a sane way (URL-driven), and thus architect our code in some meaningful way.

For the studious among us, the Compojure docs can be found at
https://github.com/weavejester/compojure/wiki.

# Creating a Compojure route

Let's do an example that will allow the awful sounding tech jargon to make sense.
We will create an extremely basic route, which will simply print out the original
request map to the screen. Let's perform the following steps:

1.  Open the `home.clj` file.

2.  Alter the `home-routes` defroute such that it looks like this:

    ```
    (defroutes home-routes
      (GET "/" [] (home-page))
      (GET "/about" [] (about-page))
      (ANY "/req" request (str request)))
    ```

3.  Start the Ring Server if it's not already started.

4.  Navigate to `http://localhost:3000/req`.

 It's possible that your Ring Server will be serving off a port other
than 3000. Check the output on `lein ring server` for the serving
port if you're unable to connect to the URL listed in step 4.

You should see something like this:

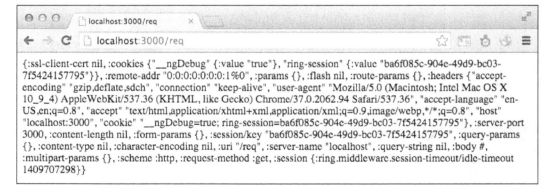

# Using defroutes

Before we dive too much into the anatomy of the routes, we should speak briefly about what `defroutes` is. The `defroutes` macro packages up all of the routes and creates one big Ring handler out of them. Of course, you don't need to define all the routes for an application under a single `defroutes` macro. You can, and should, spread them out across various namespaces and then incorporate them into the app in Luminus' `handler` namespace. Before we start making a bunch of example routes, let's move the route we've already created to its own namespace:

1.  Create a new namespace `hipstr.routes.test-routes` (`/hipstr/routes/test_routes.clj`). Ensure that the namespace makes use of the Compojure library:

    ```
    (ns hipstr.routes.test-routes
      (:require [compojure.core :refer :all]))
    ```

2.  Next, use the `defroutes` macro and create a new set of routes, and move the `/req` route we created in the `hipstr.routes.home` namespace under it:

    ```
    (defroutes test-routes
      (ANY "/req" request (str request)))
    ```

3.  Incorporate the new `test-routes` route into our application handler. In `hipstr.handler`, perform the following steps:

    1.  Add a requirement to the `hipstr.routes.test-routes` namespace:

        ```
        (:require [compojure.core :refer [defroutes]]
          [hipstr.routes.home :refer [home-routes]]
          [hipstr.routes.test-routes :refer [test-routes]]
          ...)
        ```

    2.  Finally, add the `test-routes` to the list of routes in the call to app-handler:

        ```
        (def app (app-handler
          ;; add your application routes here
          [home-routes test-routes base-routes]
        ```

We've now created and incorporated a new routing namespace. It's with this namespace where we will create the rest of the routing examples.

# Anatomy of a route

So what exactly did we just create? We created a Compojure route, which responds to any HTTP method at `/req` and returns the result of a called function, in our case a string representation of the original request map.

## Defining the method

The first component of the route defines which HTTP method the route will respond to; our route uses the ANY macro, which means our route will respond to any HTTP method. Alternatively, we could have restricted which HTTP methods the route responds to by specifying a method-specific macro. The `compojure.core` namespace provides macros for GET, POST, PUT, DELETE, HEAD, OPTIONS, and PATCH.

Let's change our route to respond only to requests made using the GET method:

```
(GET "/req" request (str request))
```

When you refresh your browser, the entire request map is printed to the screen, as we'd expect. However, if the URL and the method used to make the request don't match those defined in our route, the not-found route in `hipstr.handler/base-routes` is used. We can see this in action by changing our route to listen only to the POST methods:

```
(POST "/req" request (str request))
```

If you try and refresh the browser again, you'll notice we don't get anything back. In fact, an "HTTP 404: Page Not Found" response is returned to the client. If we POST to the URL from the terminal using `curl`, we'll get the following expected response:

```
# curl -d {} http://localhost:3000/req
{:ssl-client-cert nil, :go-bowling? "YES! NOW!", :cookies {}, :remote-
addr "0:0:0:0:0:0:0:1", :params {}, :flash nil, :route-params {},
:headers {"user-agent" "curl/7.37.1", "content-type" "application/x-
www-form-urlencoded", "content-length" "2", "accept" "*/*", "host"
"localhost:3000"}, :server-port 3000, :content-length 2, :form-params
{}, :session/key nil, :query-params {}, :content-type "application/x-
www-form-urlencoded", :character-encoding nil, :uri "/req", :server-
name "localhost", :query-string nil, :body #<HttpInput org.eclipse.
jetty.server.HttpInput@38dea1>, :multipart-params {}, :scheme :http,
:request-method :post, :session {}}
```

# Defining the URL

The second component of the route is the URL on which the route is served. This can be anything we want and as long as the request to the URL matches exactly, the route will be invoked. There are, however, two caveats we need to be aware of:

- Routes are tested in order of their declaration, so order matters.

- The trailing slash isn't handled well. Compojure will always strip the trailing slash from the incoming request but won't redirect the user to the URL without the trailing slash. As a result an HTTP 404: Page Not Found response is returned. So never base anything off a trailing slash, lest ye peril in an ocean of confusion.

# Parameter destructuring

In our previous example we directly refer to the implicit incoming request and pass that request to the function constructing the response. This works, but it's nasty. Nobody ever said, *I love passing around requests and maintaining meaningless code and not leveraging URLs*, and if anybody ever did, we don't want to work with them. Thankfully, Compojure has a rather elegant destructuring syntax.

Let's create a second route that allows us to define a request map key in the URL, then simply prints that value in the response:

```
(GET "/req/:val" [val] (str val))
```

Compojure's destructuring syntax binds HTTP request parameters to variables of the same name. In the previous syntax, the key :val will be in the request's :params map. Compojure will automatically map the value of {:params {:val...}} to the symbol val in [val]. In the end, you'll get the following output for the URL http://localhost:3000/req/holy-moly-molly:

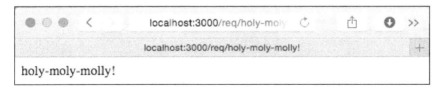

That's pretty slick but what if there is a query string? For example,
`http://localhost:3000/req/holy-moly-molly!?more=ThatsAHotTomalle`.
We can simply add the query parameter `more` to the vector, and Compojure will
automatically bring it in:

```
(GET "/req/:val" [val more] (str val "<br>" more))
```

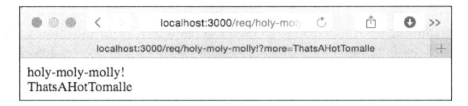

### Destructuring the request

What happens if we still need access to the entire request? It's natural to think we
could do this:

```
(GET "/req/:val" [val request] (str val "<br>" request))
```

However, `request` will always be nil because it doesn't map back to a parameter
key of the same name. In Compojure, we can use the magical `:as` key:

```
(GET "/req/:val" [val :as request] (str val "<br>" request))
```

This will now result in `request` being assigned the entire request map, as shown in
the following screenshot:

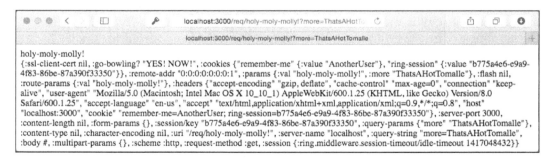

### Destructuring unbound parameters

Finally, we can bind any remaining unbound parameters into another map using `&`.
Take a look at the following example code:

```
(GET "/req/:val/:another-val/:and-another"
  [val & remainders] (str val "<br>" remainders))
```

Saving the file and navigating to `http://localhost:3000/req/holy-moly-molly!/what-about/susie-q` will render both `val` and the `map` with the remaining unbound keys `:another-val` and `:and-another`, as seen in the following screenshot:

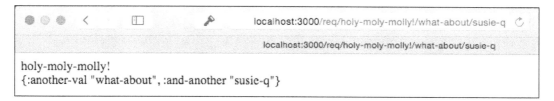

## Constructing the response

The last component in the route is the construction of the response. Whatever the third argument resolves to will be the body of our response. For example, in the following route:

```
(GET "/req/:val" [val] (str val))
```

The third component, (`str val`), will echo whatever the value passed in on the URL is.

So far, we've simply been making calls to Clojure's `str` but we can just as easily call one of our own functions. Let's add another route to our `hipstr.routes.test-routes`, and write the following function to construct its response:

```
(defn render-request-val [request-map & [request-key]]
  "Simply returns the value of request-key in request-map,
  if request-key is provided; Otherwise return the request-map.
  If request-key is provided, but not found in the request-map,
  a message indicating as such will be returned."
(str (if request-key
        (if-let [result ((keyword request-key) request-map)]
          result
          (str request-key " is not a valid key."))
        request-map)))
(defroutes test-routes
  (POST "/req" request (render-request-val request))
  ;no access to the full request map
  (GET "/req/:val" [val] (str val))
  ;use :as to get access to full request map
  (GET "/req/:val" [val :as full-req] (str val "<br>" full-req))
  ;use & to get access to the remainder of unbound symbols
  (GET "/req/:val/:another-val/:and-another" [val & remainders]
    (str val "<br>" remainders)))
```

```
;use :as to get access to unbound params, and call our route
;handler function
(GET "/req/:key" [key :as request]
  (render-request-val request key)))
```

Now when we navigate to `http://localhost:3000/req/server-port`, we'll see the value of the `:server-port` key in the request map… or wait… we should… what's wrong?

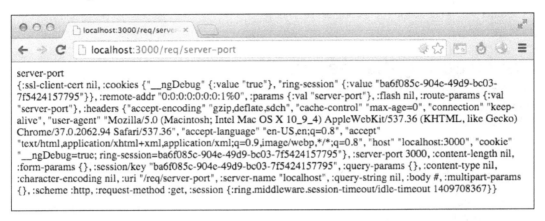

If this doesn't seem right, it's because it isn't. Why is our `/req/:val` route getting executed? As stated earlier, the order of routes is important. Because `/req/:val` with the GET method is declared earlier, it's the first route to match our request, regardless of whether or not `:val` is in the HTTP request map's parameters. Routes are matched on URL structure, not on parameters keys. As it stands right now, our `/req/:key` will never get matched. We'll have to change it as follows:

```
;use & to get access to unbound params, and call our route handler
function
(GET "/req/:val/:another-val/:and-another" [val & remainders]
  (str val "<br>" remainders))
;giving the route a different URL from /req/:val will ensure its
execution
(GET "/req/key/:key" [key :as request] (render-request-val
request key)))
```

Now that our `/req/key/:key` route is logically unique, it will be matched appropriately and render the server-port value to screen. Let's try and navigate to `http://localhost:3000/req/key/server-port` again:

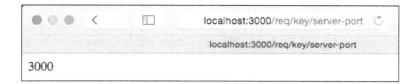

## Generating complex responses

What if we want to create more complex responses? How might we go about doing that? The last thing we want to do is hardcode a whole bunch of HTML into a function, it's not 1995 anymore, after all. This is where the Selmer library comes to the rescue.

# What is Selmer?

Selmer is a pure Clojure template system. Taking big inspiration from Django, Selmer provides a familiar syntax to one of the leading template systems in the world. With simple syntax, Selmer allows us to create text files and bind values within those files to symbols you define in Clojure. Additionally, Selmer provides syntax to perform conditional rendering, looping, template inheritance, and so on.

> Instead of covering Selmer in its entirety, we will only cover that which we need, and at the time when we need it. For a more comprehensive overview of Selmer, I encourage you to visit https://github.com/yogthos/selmer.

# Creating your first page

This is a tad misleading. Instead of creating a brand new page, we're going to modify the existing home page and cover a couple of things about Selmer along the way. But first, we need to determine where the HTML is for the home page.

Recall that our `hipstr.handler/app` uses three Ring handlers: `home-routes`, `base-routes`, and `test-routes`. We know that `test-routes` doesn't handle the home page because we just created it, and we can see that `base-routes` is defined in `hipstr.handler` and is responsible for handling "HTTP 404: Page Not Found" responses and requests to our static resources. This leaves the `home-routes`, which in hindsight, is pretty obvious given the name.

The `home-routes` handler is defined in the `hipstr.routes.home` namespace (`/src/hipstr/routes/home.clj`). The namespace defines two routes and two functions responsible for rendering each respective route's response. Notably, we see the following code right near the bottom:

```
(GET "/" [] (home-page))
```

This route serves hipstr's root page, whose content is generated by the `home-page` function.

# Rendering a page

The `home-page` function isn't doing much. In fact, all it does is call `hipstr.layout/render`, and provide the template name and a context map of values:

```
(defn home-page []
  (layout/render
  "home.html" {:content (util/md->html "/md/docs.md")}))
```

 The preceding code shines a golden nugget about Luminus: it supports rendering Markdown out of the box. This book will not get into Markdown, however, you can read about its splendid syntax at `http://daringfireball.net/projects/markdown/syntax`.

The `home.html` template in `/resources/templates/home.html` is where the visual meat of this route lives. Ultimately, it's just an HTML file with some Selmer markup. Let's discuss a few basic things about Selmer markup before we start tearing away at the template, specifically **variables**, **tags**, and **filters**.

# Variables

A templating system wouldn't be very useful if it didn't have the notion of variables. If we didn't have variables, then we'd never be able to get dynamic data into our template and then all the puppies in the world would suddenly be very, very sad.

Variables in Selmer are denoted using double curly braces, such as `{{variable-name}}`. The value of the variable is determined by a matching key in the context map passed to the template via the `layout/render` function. In the `home-route` function, explained previously, we passed a context map with a single key:

```
{:content (util/md->html "/md/docs.md")}
```

That key is now available as a Selmer variable called `content`, and we can render its HTML escaped value to the browser by sticking it between two curlies:

```
{{content}}
```

This is exactly what is happening in the `/resources/templates/home.html` file:

```
<div class="row-fluid">
  <div class="span8">
    {{content|safe}}
  </div>
</div>
```

Assuming a context map of `{:content "Hello World!"}`, the preceding fragment would actually be rendered as this:

```
<div class="row-fluid">
  <div class="span8">
    Hello World!
  </div>
</div>
```

 What's up with that `|safe` bit? We'll get to that in a bit. For now, just assume that it means you are blindly trusting that the content is nothing malicious.

Variables don't have to be flat, however, they can also be structured. For example, pretend we had the following context map:

```
{:person {:first-name "Ryan"
          :last-name "Baldwin"
          :favourite-animal "Elephant"}}
```

This would resolve to a structured Selmer variable that we could dig into using dot-notation.

```
<div class="row-fluid">
  <div class="span8">
    Hello {{person.first-name}} {{person.last-name}}!
    I see your favourite animal is the
    {{person.favourite-animal}}. How exciting!
  </div>
</div>
```

However, what happens if we try and pull the value of a variable that's not defined in the context map? For example, what if we changed the preceding code to read:

```
I see you prefer your {{person.favourite-animal}} to be {{person.
favorite-color}}. How odd.
```

Since our context map did not define a `favorite-color` key, `{{person.favorite-color}}` will simply resolve to an empty string.

# Filters

Filters are basically functions that operate over a variable's value. In our previous discussion about variables, we saw the following code:

```
{{content|safe}}
```

Here, we apply the `safe` filter to the value of `content` or, put another way, we are passing the value of `content` into the function that sits behind the `safe` filter. The result of the filter is what's subsequently rendered. In our example, `safe` restricts HTML escaping the value of `content`. So, if the value of content was something like `<h1>Hello World!</h1>`, applying the `safe` filter would render that value into the DOM verbatim, instead of HTML escaping it to `&lt;h1&gt;Hello World!&lt;/h1&gt;`.

# Filter parameters

Some filters require arguments above and beyond the value we're applying the filter to, such as the `default` filter. The `default` filter allows us to define a default value to use—other than an empty string—if the variable's value has not been set. As such, we need to provide the default filter with what we want that value to be. We do this using a colon:

```
{{content|default:"This is some default crud."}}
```

This will render the value of `content`, or if `content` is not set, render `This is some default crud.`

 You can read a complete list of Selmer's built-in filters at `https://github.com/yogthos/Selmer#built-in-filters-1`.

# Tags

Whereas variables live inside {{ }}, tags live inside {% %}. Selmer tags are something like commands or instructions. Some of them are a simple one line statement called *inline tags*, such as include. Others contain a content body (which I'll refer to as *content tags*, for the purpose of avoiding ambiguity), such as if and block. All of them, however, contain some kind of expression with varying complexity, respective to the tag.

For example, the include tag's expression is the absolute path to the file we want to include at that location in the page:

```
{% include "templates/some-other-template.html" %}
```

Comparatively, the if tag requires an expression of truthiness and a content block:

```
{% if 5 > 4 %}
  <h2>Newsflash!</h2>
  <p>Five is always bigger than 4.</p>
{% endif %}
```

In this scenario, the content block (HTML fragment) will only be rendered if the expression in the if tag evaluates to true (which it always is in our case).

 Selmer has just over a dozen different tags available at your disposal, which you can read at https://github.com/yogthos/Selmer#built-in-tags-1.

# Template inheritance

Like many templating libraries, Selmer allows a form of template inheritance. Templates can extend other templates through the use of block tags, which define a content body that can be overwritten by child templates. If we open the base.html template (/resources/templates/base.html), we see the following snippet near the middle of page:

```
<div class="container">
  {% block content %}
  {% endblock %}
</div>
```

Here, we've defined a block called content, but without any copy. The idea being that any template that inherits this template can populate this block's copy by defining block with the same name in the child. For example, say we had the following lines of code:

```
<!-- parent.html -->
<div class="example">
{% block example-content %}
{% endblock %}
</div>
<!-- child.html -->
{% extends "parent.html" %}
{% block example-content %}
Press the button to get the party started. <button>Start Party</
button>
{% endblock %}
```

If we were to render child.html, the actual output would be:

```
<div class="example">
Press the button to get the party started <button>Start Party</button>
</div>
```

However, if we were to render parent.html, the content would be empty:

```
<div class="example">
</div>
```

# Editing the home page

For our app, we don't want to have links back to the Luminus home page. We are going to modify the home page such that it behaves as a simple launch pad to either a sign up form or a login form. Open the resources/templates/home.html file and change it so that it looks like this:

```
{% extends "templates/base.html" %}
{% block content %}
  <div class="jumbotron">
    <h1>Welcome to hipstr</h1>
    <p>Obscurely building your vinyl cred since, like, now.</p>
    <p><a class="btn btn-success btn-lg"
    href="{{servlet-context}}/signup">Sign Up</a>
    or
    <a class="btn btn-primary btn-lg"
    href="{{servlet-context}}/login">Login</a></p>
  </div>
{% endblock %}
```

We see {{servlet-context}} in the preceding code. Java application containers (such as Glassfish or Tomcat) typically deploy applications at a location other than root, for example /hipstr-application. By prefixing our href sources with {{servlet-context}}, Luminus will handle the servlet context URI for us.

Save the file, refresh the screen, and be amazed at the beauty. You should see something like the following:

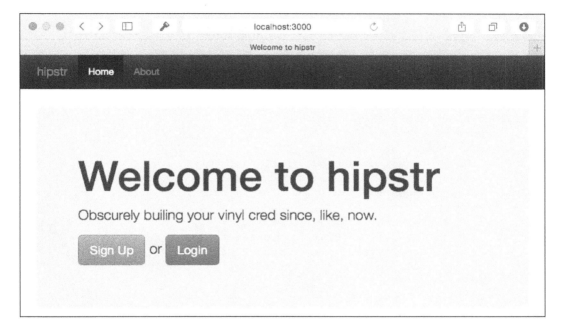

However, clicking on either of those buttons will give a 404 error. So let's create a route that can serve the sign up form.

# Serving the signup form

For now, we'll just use the existing src/hipstr/routes/home.clj file to house our route to the sign up form. Our sign up form will use the POST method to send the data to a different URL, so the route to the sign up form itself needs to be GET. Adjust hipstr.routes.home/home-routes to look like this:

```
(defroutes home-routes
  (GET "/" [] (home-page))
```

```
(GET "/about" [] (about-page))
(GET "/signup" [] "Hey there, welcome to the signup page!"))
```

Now when you save this and click the sign up button, we get a cute but completely useless salutation. So, let's get a little creative and create the actual sign up page.

# Creating the signup page

We are programmers, and therefore, we are lazy. As such, we're going to create a new template at `resources/templates/signup.html` and have it extend our base template. This way, all we need to worry about is the content of the actual login form and a heading. This is the beauty of template inheritance:

```
{% extends "templates/base.html" %}
{% block content %}
<h1>Sign Up <span class="small">Nobody will ever know.</span></h1>
<div class="row">
  <div class="col-md-6">
    <form role="form">
    <div class="form-group">
      <label for="username">Username</label>
      <input type="input" class="form-control"
      name="username" placeholder="AtticusButch">
    </div>
    <div class="form-group">
      <label for="email">Email address</label>
      <input type="email" class="form-control"
      name="email" placeholder="so1999@hotmail.com">
    </div>
    <div class="form-group">
      <label for="password">Password</label>
      <input type="password" class="form-control"
       name="password" placeholder="security-through-
       obscurity">
    </div>
    <button type="submit" class="btn
    btn-default">Submit</button>
    </form>
  </div>
</div>
{% endblock %}
```

If you save and refresh `http://localhost:300/signup`, you'll notice we still see the goofy salutation. That's because we haven't adjusted our sign up route to render the template.

Back in the `hipstr.routes.home` namespace, add a new function, `signup-page`, which is responsible for rendering the sign up page. We can use the `hipstr.layout/render` function to handle it for us:

```
(defn signup-page []
  (layout/render "signup.html"))
```

Finally, get rid of that goofy salutation in the sign up route and replace it with a call to `signup-page`:

```
(GET "/signup" [] (signup-page))
```

Now when you save and refresh, you'll see your new form:

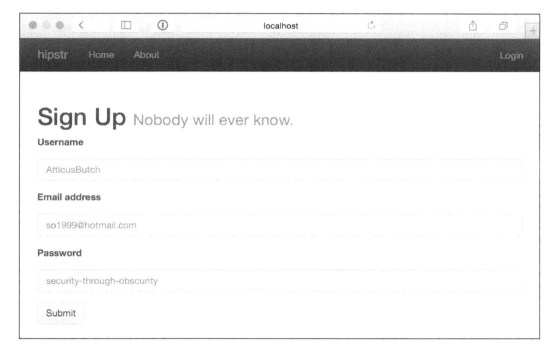

# Summary

In this chapter, you learned how to route incoming requests, extract their parameters, and pass them to Clojure functions using Compojure. You also learned how to create, render, and serve an HTML template using Selmer. We created a couple of fancy buttons and a pretty bare bones HTML form. However, currently that form doesn't do a whole lot. In the next chapter, you'll learn how to accept and validate form input. Wow! Talk about a chapter! Am I right?!

# 5
# Handling Form Input

In the previous chapter, we created a route handler to serve a sign up form. We also created the Selmer HTML template for this form, and as of now, it renders and looks pretty when we hit `http://localhost:3000/signup`. In this chapter, we're going to take it a bit further by:

- Creating an endpoint to which the form will POST
- Validating the form input
- Reporting any form validation errors back to the user
- Rendering a success template upon successful signup

## Handling the form POST

There are typically three things we need to do when handling form input: validate the input, show an error message if the input is invalid, and show a success message when the input is valid and accepted.

In order for us to validate the form input, we need to create a route where the form will POST. We made a number of these in the previous chapter, so we'll draw on that experience and pattern.

Let's create a new route for the same URL, /signup, but this time we'll ensure that it accepts a POST request instead of a GET request. We'll put it along with the existing /signup GET route in our `hipstr.routes.home` namespace:

```
(defroutes home-routes
  (GET    "/"        []        (home-page))
  (GET    "/about"   []        (about-page))
  (GET    "/signup"  []        (signup-page))
  (POST   "/signup"  [& form]  (str "nice job")))
```

We now have two routes for the same URL, one that will handle the GET request, and another that will handle the POST request. You'll notice that GET doesn't care about any parameters, however, POST uses Compojure's *get the rest of the request map* parameters destructuring syntax. This is just a bit of semantic sugar so that it's clear that we're working with just the values posted from the form instead of the entire request map.

That being said, the POST route doesn't do a whole lot for us at this point other than giving us a slightly sarcastic "nice job". Let's create a function similar to the existing `hipstr.routes.home/signup-page` function to handle the POST /signup response.

First, we need to make use of the `ring.util.response` namespace, as it has a function to issue a response redirect, which we can use to redirect the user to a sign up success page. Add the following to the `hipster.routes.home` namespace's :require key:

```
[ring.util.response :as response]
```

Next, we'll write the function to determine the appropriate response:

```
(defn signup-page-submit [user]
  #_(let [errors (signup/validate-signup user)]
    (if (empty? errors)
      (response/redirect "/signup-success")
      (layout/render "signup.html" (assoc user :errors errors)))))
```

In the preceding function, we validate the form using the `hipstr.signup` namespace (which we'll create next) and then, if successful, redirect the user to a sign up success page; otherwise, we repopulate the form and display the validation errors.

 For now we've commented out the `let` form, so that we can compile and refresh our pages as often as we like until the `signup` namespace is implemented.

Before we create the `hipstr.signup` namespace, let's quickly change our route handler to make use of the `signup-page-submit` function and add a route for the success page:

```
(defroutes home-routes
  (GET    "/"       []        (home-page))
  (GET    "/about"  []        (about-page))
  (GET    "/signup" []        (signup-page))
  (POST   "/signup" [& form]  (signup-page-submit form))
  (GET "/signup-success" []   "Success!"))
```

# Validating the form POST

We might write perfect code but, unfortunately, our users are mere mortals and thus are prone to giving us cruddy data by mistake. If you recall, in *Chapter 1*, *Getting Started with Luminus*, we used the Luminus template to generate the hipstr application, which includes the lib-noir library for us. One of the helper namespaces provided by lib-noir is a noir.validation namespace.

## The noir.validation namespace

The noir.validation namespace provides methods to validate data in a variety of ways. It includes functions to check whether or not an input is nil, is an e-mail, is of a certain minimum length, and so on. This is excellent because I hate writing validation code, and I'm sure you do, too.

However, while noir.validation has a lot of functions that can be used to validate data, its actual validation framework makes some unfortunate assumptions as to how it will be used. It is also stateful, which makes it difficult to test and, frankly, is pretty unnecessary for a validation framework.

Instead of depending on the framework of noir.validation and its way of doing things, we're going to use some of its validation functions in conjunction with Validateur.

## The Validateur library

The Validateur library is an alternative validation library to noir.validation. Using Validateur, we can define a collection of validators as a single function, which you can then apply against a map of key/values to be validated. The function will then return a map of all keys in the map that failed the validation and for each invalid key, a set of messages detailing why the validation failed (which is slightly similar to noir.validation but without all the evils of maintaining the state). The validators that we'll construct with Validateur are easily reusable and composable with other validators.

> The website of Validateur will provide a lot of information to you. The library is well documented and available for your perusal at http://clojurevalidations.info/.

# Adding the Validateur dependency

The first thing that we need to do, as is the case with any third-party library we want to use, is import the library in our `project.clj` file as a dependency of the app. Adjust the project's dependencies vector so it is similar to this:

```
(defproject...
  :dependencies [[org.clojure/clojure "1.6.0]
                        ;...snipped for brevity
                        [com.november/validateur "2.3.1"]]
  ;...rest of our project...
```

# Creating the user validation namespace

It can sometimes be difficult to determine where exactly one should write the validation code. Because one of the strengths of `Validateur` is that validators can be created, reused, and composed together to create more complex validators, it makes sense for us to create the validators in appropriate namespaces.

In our case, the sign up form has three fields that require validation: `:username`, `:email`, and `:password`. However, if we were to further extend this application to have something like a password reset form, then the e-mail and username validators would come in handy. As such, let's create a new namespace called `hipstr.validators.user` and put our validators in it.

Create a new directory in our `/src/hipstr` directory called `validators`:

```
# mkdir validators
```

Create a new `hipstr.validators.user-validator` namespace and ensure that it uses the `validateur.validation` namespace:

```
(ns hipstr.validators.user-validator
  (:require [validateur.validation :refer :all]))
```

The key function in `validateur.validation` is the `validation-set`. The `validation-set` function can be thought of as a factory responsible for creating and returning the actual validator to be applied to a map. The `validation-set` function accepts a list of rules, which will ultimately be used to validate a map. The validator returns a set of error messages for any key whose value is invalid, otherwise it returns an empty map.

# Validating required fields

We can create a simple validator that checks for required fields using the `presence-of` function rule:

```
(defn validate-signup [signup]
  "Validates the incoming map of values from our signup form,
   and returns a set of error messages for any invalid key.
   Expects signup to have :username, :email, and :password."
  (let [v (validation-set                          ;#1
    (presence-of #{:username :email :password}))]  ;#2
    (v signup)))
```

In the preceding code, we created our own little `validate-signup` function, which will take the parameters map from our POST/signup up route. At #1, we construct our validator by calling `validation-set`, and we pass it to our first rule, `presence-of` (as shown on #2), which itself accepts the set of keys that must be present, and truthy, in the map to be deemed valid (in our case, the sign-up map).

Ultimately, `presence-of` returns a function (as do all the rules we pass to validation-set), which will be used by `validation-set` during validation. These functions accept a map to be validated and perform their task against that map. We can take a peek into this at the REPL:

```
# lein repl
hipstr.repl=> (require '[validateur.validation :refer :all])

nil

hipstr.repl => (let [presence-of-fn (presence-of
        #=>   #{:username :email :password})]
        #=>   (presence-of-fn {:username "TheDude"}))
[false {:password #{"can't be blank"}, :email #{"can't be blank"}}]
```

In the preceding REPL code, we load the `validateur.validation` namespace and assign the result of `presence-of` to our own function `presence-of-fn`. We call `presence-of-fn` and pass it the map to be validated. The validation fails because `:password` and `:email` are not provided.

It's easy to see how `validation-set` simply iterates blindly over all of its validators, forwarding the map to each validator in question. Its simplicity is beautiful and elegant.

If we were to call `validate-signup` from the REPL with an invalid map, we'd see the following:

```
hipstr.repl=> (use '[hipstr.validators.user-validator])
nil
hipstr.repl=> (validate-signup {:username "TheDude"})
{:email #{"can't be blank"}, :password #{"can't be blank"}}
hipstr.repl=> (validate-signup {:username "TheDude"
  :email "thedude@bides.net" :password "12345678"})
{}
```

The default error message for `presence-of` is `"can't be blank"`, however, we can provide our own message by passing the `:message` keyword argument. Adjust the `presence-of`'s arguments to look like the following:

```
(presence-of #{:username :email :password}
  :message "is a required field")
```

If we re-execute from the REPL, we'll now see a different error message:

```
hipstr.repl=> (use 'hipstr.validators.user-validator :reload)
nil
hipstr.repl=> (validate-signup {:username "TheDude"})
{:email #{"is a required field."}, :password #{"is a required
field."}}
```

# Validating the format

Of course, checking for required fields isn't the only thing we need to ensure. We also need to ensure whatever values are supplied are in the correct format. I'm making the executive decision that our application will only allow a limited set of characters for usernames, because I'm old and grumbly.

We can use the `format-of` rule to ensure that a given value is appropriately formatted. Because the validator returned by `validation-set` chains all the validation rules together, we can add the `format-of` rule after the `presence-of` rule. Adjust `validate-signup` to be similar to the following:

```
;...snipped for brevity...
(let [v (validation-set
          (presence-of #{:username :email :password)
                        :message "is a required field.")
          (format-of :username
                      :format #"^[a-zA-Z0-9_]*$"
              :message "Only letters, numbers, and underscores
allowed."))])
```

The `format-of` rule accepts the key whose value's format is to be validated (`:username`), a regex pattern to which the value must conform, and an optional message if we don't want to use the default one provided (which in the case of `format-of` is `"has incorrect format"`).

Many of these functions take additional, optional parameters but for the sake of brevity, we aren't covering the entire suite. You can, as always, check out the docs at `http://reference. clojurevalidations.info/validateur.validation. html#var-compose-sets`.

At this point, if we try to validate our test data from the last example, we'll get the following response:

```
hipstr.repl=> (validate-signup {:username "The Dude"
:email "thedude@bides.net" :password "12345678"})
{:username #{"Only letters, numbers, and underscores allowed."}}
```

Excellent! So our format validator is working, but what happens if we don't pass `:username` at all:

```
hipstr.repl=> (validate-signup
  {:email "thedude@bides.net" :password "12345678"})
=> {:username #{"is a required field" "can't be blank."}}
```

Huh, now that's interesting. Why did we get multiple required/blank validation messages for `:username`? Our first validator, `presence-of`, failed, so the message we provided was added to the error set for `:username`. In addition, `format-of` also does a check to ensure that the value is provided and adds its own validation message to the error set, `can't be blank`. Considering `format-of` already has its own check for existence, we may as well remove `:username` from `presence-of`, and change the default message for blank value validation in `format-of`:

```
;...snipped for brevity...
(let [v (validation-set
          (presence-of #{:email :password}
                  :message "is a required field.")
          (format-of :username
                  :format #"^[a-zA-Z0-9_]*$"
                  :message "Only letters, numbers, and
                                  underscores allowed."
                  :blank-message "is a required field"))])
```

Next up, we'll verify the password.

# Validating length of values

At this point, you might be starting to see a pattern, and it might come as no surprise that along with `presence-of` and `format-of`, there also exists `length-of`. The `length-of` rule can either check for an exact length or a range. Because we are software developers and know the importance of good passwords, we'll want a minimum length and a rather large maximum length. Let's add the `length-of` rule to the list of rules in the `validation-set`:

```
;…snipped for brevity…
(length-of :password
           :within (range 8 101)
           :message-fn
             (fn [type m attribute & args]
               (if (= type :blank)
                 "is a required field"
                 "Passwords must be between 8
                  and 100 characters long.")))
```

In `length-of` we provided `:within`, which accepts a range. Alternatively, we could have specified an exact value using `:is`. The major difference between `length-of` and the other rules we've used so far is the `:message-fn` argument. Because `length-of` can fail for multiple reasons—it could fall outside our range, or not meet the exact value (if we had provided one), or be altogether blank—we can pass a function that determines the appropriate error message to return. From the docs:

> *:message-fn (default nil): function to retrieve message with signature (fn [type m attribute & args]). type will be :length:is or :length:within, args will be the applied number or range*

Unfortunately, the docs are slightly misleading, as `type` can also have the value `:blank`. Hence, our `:message-fn` function will return a "is a required field" message if the `type` is `:blank`, otherwise it will return a message that covers the rest the validation cases appropriately.

Lastly, we'll take a look at one more rule function to help us validate the format of our e-mail address.

# Validation predicates

E-mail addresses are hard to validate. Their regular expressions are difficult to maintain, ugly, and I'd rather let some other underlying library validate the e-mail address for me. Thankfully, one of the rules we can use is `validate-with-predicate`.

The `validate-with-predicate` rule takes a predicate and returns whatever the predicate returns. We can leverage this in conjunction with the `noir.validation/is-email?` function to validate the e-mail.

First, add the `noir.validation` requirement to the namespace:

```
(ns hipstr.validators.user
  (:require [validateur.validation :refer :all]
  [noir.validation :as v]))
```

Next, add the `validate-with-predicate` rule to `validation-set`, which will determine whether the e-mail is in the correct format:

```
;...snipped for brevity...
  (validate-with-predicate :email
#(v/is-email? (:email %))                ;#1
:message-fn                              ;#2
  (fn [validation-map]
    (if (v/has-value? (:email validation-map))
      "The email's format is incorrect"
      "is a required field")))
```

At #1, we define the predicate that will be used for this rule, which is just an anonymous function that passes the sign up map to the `noir.validation/is-email?` function. The interesting bit takes place at #2. Because `validate-with-predicate` has no idea how the passed map is being validated, or why validation failed, we provide a `:message-fn` funtion, which takes the entire map. We can then use the map to determine why the validation failed, and thus return an appropriate message. In our case, we know the e-mail's format is incorrect if a value was provided, otherwise we know it's blank. Our `:message-fn` will simply return an appropriate message for the two cases.

At this point, the `validate-signup` function should look like this:

```
(defn validate-signup [signup]
  "Validates the incoming map of values from our signup form,
   and returns a set of error messages for any invalid key.
   Expects signup to have :username, :email, and :password."
  (let [v (validation-set
            (presence-of #{:email :password}
                         :message "is a required field.")
            (format-of :username
                       :format #"^[a-zA-Z0-9_]*$"
                       :message "Only letters, numbers, and
                                 underscores allowed."
```

```
                             :blank-message "is a required field")
                 (length-of :password
                             :within (range 8 101)
                             :message-fn (fn [type m attribute & args]
                                          (if (= type :blank)
                                            "is a required field"
                                            "Password must be between 8
                                                      and 100 characters
long.")))
                 (validate-with-predicate :email
                   #(v/is-email? (:email %))
                   :message-fn (fn [validation-map]
                                 (if (v/has-value?
                                       (:email validation-map))
                                   "the email's format is incorrect"
                                   "is a required field")))))]
        (v signup)))
```

 Sometimes code formatting in a book is difficult to read. Here's a link to a gist to give your eyes a break: `http://bit.ly/1rHZB0E`

"But hold on! At the start of this section, you said that using `Validateur` allows us to compose reusable validators! This `validate-signup` can't be reused by anything but the signup form!" you may say. You are correct and we can fix this.

## Making reusable validators

So far, we've created one big validator using the `validateur.validation/validation-set` function. It works, but it's monolithic and can't be used by anything other than the signup form, which is unfortunate.

To open this up, we can use `validateur.validation/compose-sets`, which instead of taking a collection of validator rules, takes a collection of validators returned by `validateur.validation/validation-set`. This allows us to extract each of the validator rules in the `validate-signup` function into its own validator using `validation-set`, thus allowing us to reuse a single validator wherever we want.

First, let's extract each rule in the `validate-signup` function into its own validator, such that our code looks like this:

```
(ns hipstr.validators.user
  (:require [validateur.validation :refer :all]
            [noir.validation :as v]))
```

```
(def email-validator
 (validation-set
  (validate-with-predicate :email
    #(v/is-email? (:email %))
    :message-fn
      (fn [validation-map]
        (if (v/has-value? (:email validation-map))
          "The email's format is incorrect"
          "is a required field")))))

(def username-validator
  (validation-set
    (format-of :username
            :format #"^[a-zA-Z0-9_]*$"
            :blank-message "is a required field"
            :message "Only letters, numbers, and
                            underscores allowed.")))
(def password-validator
  (validation-set
    (length-of :password
            :within (range 8 101)
            :blank-message "is a required field."
            :message-fn (fn [type m attribute & args]
                       (if (= type :blank)
                         "is a required field"
                         "Passwords must be between 8
                         and 100 characters long.")))))

(defn validate-signup [signup]
  "Validates the incoming signup map and returns a set of error
  messages for any invalid field."
  (let [v (validation-set)]
    (v signup)))
```

In the previous code snippet, we created a single validator for each of our rules. Each of these validators can now be used by anything we want. Of course, now our `validate-signup` doesn't really do anything. However, we can change this by swapping out `validation-set` with `compose-sets`, passing each of the previously defined validators and then immediately invoking it.

```
(defn validate-signup [signup]
  "Validates the incoming signup map and returns a set of error
  messages for any invalid field."
  ((compose-sets email-validator username-validator
password-validator) signup))
```

A gist of the entire refactored namespace is available at http://bit.ly/1CsSrrd.

Our individual validators are now reusable and we can compose complex validators from them. Now, we just have to report errors to the user for any of the failed validations, or redirect them to the success page.

# Reporting errors to the user

We already set up our route handler at the start of this chapter, such that, if there were any errors, we would re-render the signup.html page with the user's submitted data along with the errors. Since we're using Selmer to render our templates, and because Selmer gracefully handles nil to be an empty string, we can safely treat user's data and reported errors as though they were present.

Adjust the signup.html page such that it looks like this:

```
{% extends "templates/base.html" %}
{% block content %}
<h1>Sign Up <span class="small">Nobody will ever know.</span></h1>
<div class="row">
  <div class="col-md-6">
    <form role="form" method="post">
      <div class="form-group">
        <label for="username">Username</label>
          <ul class="errors">
            {% for e in errors.username %}        <!-- #1 -->
              <li>{{e}}</li>
            {% endfor %}
          </ul>
          <input type="input" name="username" class="form-control"
          id="username" placeholder="AtticusButch"
        value="{{username}}">
      </div>
      <div class="form-group">
        <label for="email">Email address</label>
        <ul class="errors">
          {% for e in errors.email %}
          <li>{{e}}</li>
          {% endfor %}
        </ul>
      <input type="email" name="email" class="form-control"
      id="email" placeholder="so1999@hotmail.com"
      value="{{email}}">
```

```
      </div>
      <div class="form-group">
        <label for="password">Password</label>
        <ul class="errors">
          {% for e in errors.password %}
          <li>{{e}}</li>
          {% endfor %}
        </ul>
        <input type="password" name="password"
        class="form-control" id="password"
        placeholder="security-through-obscurity">
      </div>
      <button type="submit" class="btn btn-default">Submit
      </button>
    </form>
  </div>
</div>
{% endblock %}
```

We are using Selmer's *cycle* tag (as shown at #1) — which is actually a `for` loop — to loop through any errors that exist for a given field and render out a fragment of HTML. We can do this because the validator that we created returns a set of error messages for any key whose validation failed; otherwise an empty map is returned, which Selmer can gracefully handle. We also were able to render out each respective input's value, if the user had already submitted one (so that they don't have to fill it in again, which would lead to them raging).

Finally, let's modify the `hipstr.routes.home` namespace and the `signup-page-submit` route handler we created, to make use of this validator.

First, add our `user-validator` to the list of requirements as follows:

```
(:require ;...snipped for brevity...
    [hipstr.validators.user-validator :as v])
```

Then uncomment the `let` form in our `signup-page-submit`, and change the `signup` alias to be v instead:

```
(defn signup-page-submit [user]
  (let [errors (v/validate-signup user)]
    (if (empty? errors)
      (response/redirect "/signup-success")
      (layout/render "signup.html" (assoc user :errors errors)))))
```

The preceding Selmer template will now render the following page when any validation errors are present:

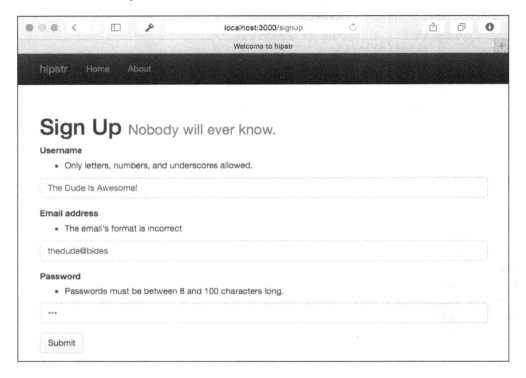

Finally, let's add a **Cascade Style Sheet** (**CSS**) style so that our error messages are a deeply foreboding red. CSS styles are stored in the /resources/public/css folder. Out of the box, Luminus generates a screen.css file for us, prewired and ready to go. We'll add our style to it:

```
.errors {
  padding-left: 20px;
  color: red;
}
```

Save the file and refresh, and you'll have some urgent looking messages.

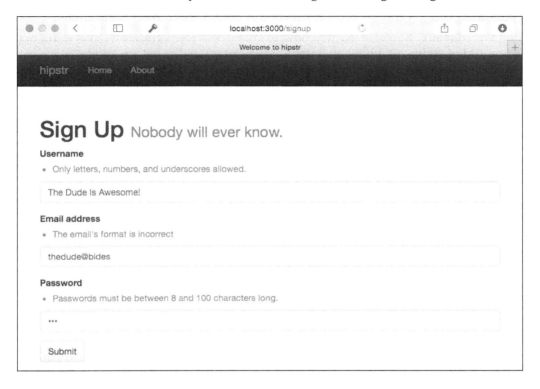

Finally, once we provide a valid username, e-mail, and password, we'll be redirected to the /signup-success route, and our simple little message will be displayed:

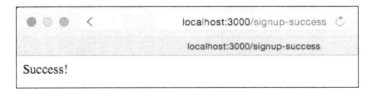

# Summary

In this chapter, you learned how to accept and validate, submitted input from a user using `Validateur`. You also learned how to create reusable validators, thus reducing the amount of code you'd have to write in the future. Finally, we adjusted our `signup.html` template to use a new Selmer tag—the cycle tag—to loop through our errors and render each one out appropriately. However, we lived a little dangerously: we did some refactoring, but had no way of ensuring that what we refactored worked until we tested it in the browser. In the next chapter, we'll take a look at how we could have written some tests to validate this for us.

# 6
# Testing in Clojure

Testing is quite possibly the most controversial topic in software development I've ever seen. Some developers are passionate about the merits of automated testing, what should be tested, and how. Conversely, some developers are dead set against automated testing. This can be especially so in languages that come with a REPL. That being said, Clojure still ships with a `clojure.test` namespace. As such, this chapter will focus primarily on how we can use `clojure.test` to write tests for our `hipstr.validators.user` namespace. In this chapter, we will:

- Explore the necessity of automated testing in Clojure (hint: I believe there is always room for testing)
- Discuss how to write assertions and tests, and how to run them

 What this chapter won't cover, however, is extensive philosophy, patterns, and so on. Automated testing is a huge topic, one that I've studied for over ten years, and still have an enormous amount to learn. The purpose of this chapter is to show you enough to get going: to provide you with a starting point from which you may branch out.

Buckle up, this chapter will likely produce some disagreements.

 There are more testing frameworks for Clojure than you can possibly imagine. While this chapter will focus on the `clojure.test` namespace that ships with Clojure, you might want something a little more fancy. You can see a high-level overview of various Clojure testing libraries at https://clojure-libraries.appspot.com/cat/Testing.

# The necessity of testing

I will fully admit that, for the bulk of my career, I've used automated testing in some capacity on almost every project I've worked on. For nearly a decade, I've employed the practice of **test-driven development** (**TDD**) to some degree.

While working on applications using Java or .NET, I often write tests to help me explore ideas and assist in the design and implementation of those ideas. I follow the TDD "Red/Green/Refactor" (`http://en.wikipedia.org/wiki/Test-driven_development#Development_style`) with discipline, and what I produce often works, is extensible, and is in the style of those languages (for better or for worse). I also have a safety net, which validates whether the system does what it is supposed to do; this comes in handy as the system grows, changes, and gets refactored over time.

The Red/Green/Refactor methodology dictates that you write a failing test first, then implement the least amount of code to get that test to pass, and then refactor your code (both the code that you're testing, as well as the test itself). The following diagram illustrates this process:

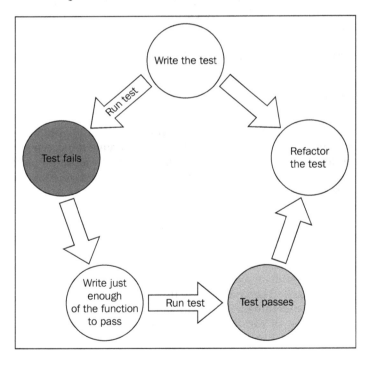

This methodology works well for Java and .NET applications, as well as any application that has a compiling step in the build process, which prohibits us from being able to test the function *inline* while we develop it.

However, when working with languages such as Python, JavaScript, or Clojure, wherein a shell/console/REPL exists and is at my disposal, my practice changes. In Clojure, I will start writing the function first, and will use the REPL to validate the results of the function. Once I'm satisfied with the result of the function, I then write the tests. Sometimes, I'll toggle back and forth between the REPL and the test, writing the test for each scenario I attempt in the REPL. I'll repeat this process for any refactors I make to the function under test, as well. The following diagram illustrates this somewhat more streamlined process:

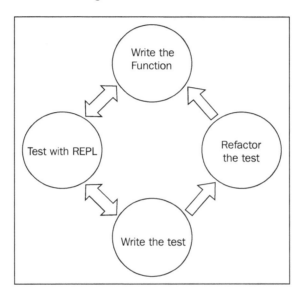

This process works particularly well if you're using an editor such as Light Table. One of the great features in Light Table is called InstaREPL, wherein you can convert any Clojure file you're working on into a REPL and get live feedback on everything happening in the module while you type. Function results, variable values, and exceptions appear inline with your code. The result is an incredibly immersive development experience and the turnaround time on feedback is approximately zero.

The following is a screenshot of Light Table's InstaREPL in action while developing the `hipstr.validators.user-validator` namespace in *Chapter 5, Handling Form Input*.

```
user_validator.clj*  x

1   (ns hipstr.validators.user-validator
2     (:require [noir.validation :as v]
3               [validateur.validation :refer :all])) nil
4
5   (def email-validator fn
6     (validation-set
7       (validate-with-predicate :email
8                     #(v/is-email? (:email %))
9                     :message-fn (fn [validation-map] {:email "thedude@bides"}
10                           (if (v/has-value? (:email validation-map)) {:email "thedude@bides"}
11                             "The email's format is incorrect"
12                             "is a required field")))))
13
14  (email-validator {:email "thedude@bides"}) {:email #{"The email's format is incorrect"}}
```

Some developers argue that using the REPL is the only thing required when developing in Clojure, as it allows them to validate the results of their function and proceed after they get what they want. However, this does not address the ongoing maintenance, especially in teams where more than one person is working on the code base or in an environment employing continuous integration, where running tests is typically a step in the build process.

# Anatomy of a test

There are three macros in the `clojure.test` namespace, which are the trifecta of testing in Clojure: `deftest`, `is`, and `testing`. These three macros are explained as follows:

- `deftest`: This is similar to `def` or `defn` and defines our test function. Tests may call other tests, however, this is a practice that I consider dangerous, as it can result in fragile tests that are, by their nature, rather difficult to debug.

  Usage: (`deftest name & body`)

- `is`: This is used to make an assertion in our test. The predicate we pass to `is` should return a Boolean. We can also optionally provide a message, which will be attached to the assertion and displayed as part of the failure written to `stdout`.

  Usage: (`is form`)

  (`is form message`)

`is` also allows the following two special forms that can be used to check for exceptions:

○ `thrown?`: This is used to ensure that an exception of a specific type is thrown, and if not, fails the test.

Usage: (`thrown? e form`)

Here's an example of this form:

```
(is (thrown? InvocationTargetException
              (an-unsound-function)))
```

○ `thrown-with-msg?`: This does the same as `thrown`, but additionally asserts that the exception's message matches a regular expression.

Usage: (`thrown-with-msg? e regex form`)

Here's an example of this form:

```
(is (thrown-with-msg? InvocationTargetException
  #"StackOverflowError" (an-unsound-function)))
```

- `testing`: This allows us to provide an additional context to the list of testing contexts within a test function. Testing contexts can be nested, but the root testing context must reside inside `deftest`.

Usage: (`testing string & body`)

Here's an example of this form:

```
(deftest some-cool-tests
  (testing "a testing context:"
    (testing "a nested testing context"
      (let [some-val 6]
        (is (some #{some-val} (range 1 10)))))))
```

> Note that the `clojure.test` namespace is by no means limited to just these three macros. For a comprehensive list of functionalities of `clojure.test`, refer to the docs at `https://clojure.github.io/clojure/clojure.test-api.html`.

While the preceding macros allow you to create a range of tests and save you some typing, ultimately, I think they produce poor output. When a test fails, we don't want to have to think "Huh, I wonder what went wrong?" We should, ideally, know exactly what went wrong. If we change the value of some-val from 6 to 10, the test will fail, producing the following output:

```
hipstr — bash — Solarized Dark ansi — 88×15
                              bash                                          +
ryanbaldwin@slim-2:~/dev/hipstr$ lein test hipstr.test.validators.user-validator-test

lein test hipstr.test.validators.user-validator-test

lein test :only hipstr.test.validators.user-validator-test/some-cool-tests

FAIL in (some-cool-tests) (user_validator_test.clj:8)
a testing context: a nested testing context
expected: (some #{some-val} (range 1 10))
  actual: (not (some #{10} (1 2 3 4 5 6 7 8 9)))

Ran 1 tests containing 1 assertions.
1 failures, 0 errors.
Tests failed.
ryanbaldwin@slim-2:~/dev/hipstr$
```

This is somewhat useful. However, I prefer each test to assert something specific, and for the test name to be a statement of fact. There's nothing worse than seeing a failing test where the output message is FAIL in (test-service). What failed in the service? What were we actually testing? The "statement-of-fact" as a test name tends to:

- Keep our tests focused
- Produce output that makes a bit more sense

Let's change our preceding example test to not use any testing contexts, and instead use a simple deftest with a statement of fact, but keep the value at 10 so that the test fails:

```
(deftest test-value-must-fall-between-1-and-9
  (let [some-val 10]
    (is (some #{some-val} (range 1 10)))))
```

This test will now produce the following output when it fails:

```
● ● ●                    hipstr — bash — Solarized Dark ansi — 88×15
                                      bash                                      +
ryanbaldwin@slim-2:~/dev/hipstr$ lein test hipstr.test.validators.user-validator-test

lein test hipstr.test.validators.user-validator-test

lein test :only hipstr.test.validators.user-validator-test/test-value-must-fall-between-
1-and-9

FAIL in (test-value-must-fall-between-1-and-9) (user_validator_test.clj:6)
expected: (some #{some-val} (range 1 10))
  actual: (not (some #{10} (1 2 3 4 5 6 7 8 9)))

Ran 1 tests containing 1 assertions.
1 failures, 0 errors.
Tests failed.
ryanbaldwin@slim-2:~/dev/hipstr$ ▊
```

Of course, you can name and write your tests however you want, I do not judge. I've found in my experience, however, that the "statement-of-fact-test-name" convention, despite creating lengthy test names, tends to produce focused tests, resulting in less confusion and frustration when a test inevitably fails.

# Writing and running our first test

We're going to create a few tests for the validators we created in *Chapter 5, Handling Form Input*. In our directory structure, we have the src and test directories. I'll give you two seconds to determine under which directory our tests should go... got it? If you said src, then I have failed to achieve the modest task that was my charge. We will be storing our tests in the test directory using the following steps:

1. Create a directory in the /test/hisptr/test directory called validators.

2. Create a file in the /text/hipstr/test/validators directory called user_ validator_test.clj.

3. In user_validator_test.clj, define our namespace and include the clojure.test namespace and the namespace we wish to test—in our case, the hipstr.validators.user-validator namespace:

   ```
   (ns hipstr.test.validators.user-validator-test
     (:require [hipstr.validators.user-validator :as uv])
     (:use clojure.test))
   ```

4. Next, let's add a test that ensures only one error message is returned in the errors map when an e-mail address is blank:

```
(deftest only-1-error-message-returned-when-email-is-blank
  (let [result (:email (uv/email-validator {:email ""}))]
    (is (= 1 (count result)))))
```

Save the file, open the terminal, and we'll run the test.

# Running tests

Running tests is dead easy using the Leiningen test task. The lein test task, when run by itself, will run all tests under the hipstr.test namespace. Alternatively, we can provide one or more namespaces that we wish to isolate test execution to, which, for now, we will use. Open your terminal, navigate to the root of your source tree, and tell Leiningen to run all the tests in the hipstr.test.validators.user-validator-test namespace:

```
hipstr — bash — Solarized Dark ansi — 86×7
                           bash                              +
ryanbaldwin@slim-2:~/dev/hipstr$ lein test hipstr.test.validators.user-validator-test

lein test hipstr.test.validators.user-validator-test

Ran 1 tests containing 1 assertions.
0 failures, 0 errors.
ryanbaldwin@slim-2:~/dev/hipstr$ 
```

The output indicates that it ran one test containing a single assertion, and that it passed. This is great, as this is the test and assertion that we wrote. Manually running tests can become cumbersome over time. Thankfully, there are plugins to automate this for us.

# Running tests automatically

While using lein test gets the job done, it has some drawbacks, most notably you have to manually run the tests (which becomes annoying) and it has a slow start up time. Instead of being a prisoner of our own development, we can break the shackles of keystrokes using the lein quickie plugin.

The lein quickie plugin will watch our code, and anytime it detects a change (save), all the tests in our classpath whose namespaces include our project name and end in test, will be re-evaluated. It even produces a green or red bar indicating whether our tests successfully passed or failed.

To install and use the `lein quickie` plugin, perform the following steps:

1. Add the plugin to the `project.clj` file's `:plugins` list, as follows:

```
:plugins [[lein-ring "0.8.13"]
   [lein-environ "1.0.0"]
   [lein-ancient "0.5.5"]
   [quickie "0.3.6"]]
```

2. In the terminal, refresh your dependencies by doing a `lein deps`.

3. Still in the terminal, run `lein quickie`. The plugin will scan for all your tests, run them, and start watching for changes.

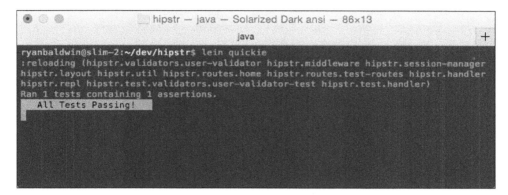

If you make a quick change to the `user-validators-test` namespace (say, insert a space and hit save), the `lein quickie` plugin will automatically detect the change and re-run the tests.

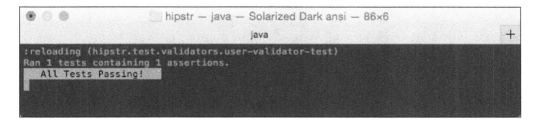

Finally, you can quit `lein quickie` session at anytime by hitting *Ctrl + C*.

There are more options you can incorporate to run tests with `lein quickie`, such as limiting the scope of which tests are validated. Take a look at the `lein quickie` docs at `https://github.com/jakepearson/quickie`.

# Refactoring tests

Let's write another test, which ensures that the sole message returned indicates that the e-mail is a required field. Full caveat: I don't typically like writing tests, which test copy (content) because copy tends to change almost every day. Testing for copy is one of the biggest testing pain points I've seen on teams over the years, and I don't believe that its value outweighs manual testing (in fact, I think it has an overall negative value due to the maintenance overhead). However, because our e-mail validator can return different messages depending on what went wrong, we should ensure that it returns the correct message. Add the following test, which ensures that the appropriate message is returned when an e-mail is not provided:

```
(deftest blank-email-returns-email-is-required-message
  (let [result (:email (uv/email-validator {:email ""}))]
    (is (= "is a required field" (first result)))))
```

If you save and run this test (or just save, if you're using `lein quickie`), you'll see that it passes. That's great. What isn't so great is that we have the same code written in each test, and code we'll likely need to use for subsequent e-mail validation tests, that sets up the result value. Let's create a simple function that validates an e-mail address for us, and then returns the `:email` errors in the validator result map, as follows:

```
(defn validate-email [email]
  "Validates the provided email for us, and returns the
   set of validation messages for the email, if any."
  (:email (email-validator {:email email})))
```

With the `validate-email` function, we can now change the `let` form in each of our tests to be as follows:

```
(let [result (validate-email "")] )
```

The test is now a bit easier to read. We can do one more refactoring before moving on. Because the two tests are so similar (we are only expecting one message back, and that message is expected to have a certain value), we can move the two assertions into the same test. Move the assertion in `only-1-error-message-returned-when-email-is-blank` into `blank-email-returns-email-is-required-message`, and then delete the `only-1-error` test:

```
(deftest blank-email-returns-email-is-required-message
  (let [result (validate-email "")]
    (is (= 1 (count result)))
    (is (= "is a required field" (first result)))))
```

While we typically want to keep our tests focused and avoid issuing a lot of assertions, moving the two assertions into a single `deftest`, in this case, works because asserting a single error message exists is a precursor to asserting the actual message itself.

At this point, you should have the hang of it. There's no real magic to writing unit tests in Clojure. We will leave the validator tests for now and move on to how we can do integration tests using `clojure.test` and Ring.

 View the entire `hipstr.test.validators.user-validator-test` namespace at `http://bit.ly/11FI8PX`, as well as its impact on refactoring the `hipstr.validators.user-validator` namespace at `http://bit.ly/1Cvui3n`.

# Writing a high-level integration test

I've always been weary of writing integration tests in the manner of unit tests because when they fail they're difficult to diagnose. All that a failed unit-style integration test tells us is that something, somewhere, broke down. In an ideal world, you would also have a unit test, which when an integration test fails, will also fail. However, rare is the team filled with unit test passion such that a beautiful pairing of failures exist. So, while we will see how we can use James Reeves' `ring-mock` to do a full-fledged integration test, we must also keep in mind that integration tests on their own are not enough.

For this example, we are going to add an additional test to the `hipstr.test.handler` namespace that was generated by Luminus when we generated our project. You'll see something like this:

```
(ns hipstr.test.handler
  (:use clojure.test
        ring.mock.request
        hipstr.handler))

(deftest test-app
  (testing "main route"
    (let [response (app (request :get "/"))]
      (is (= 200 (:status response)))))

  (testing "not-found route"
    (let [response (app (request :get "/invalid"))]
      (is (= 404 (:status response))))))
```

We've not executed any of the tests from this namespace yet, but if you recall, simply running the `lein test`, without specifying any namespaces will run all tests under the `hipstr.test` namespace. Alternatively, if you change the namespace to end in `test`, the `lein quickie` plugin will also execute it.

# Using ring.mock.request

The only real difference between how we construct the integration tests and the unit tests is that we use the `ring.mock.request` function. This function will actually construct a valid request map for the given HTTP method and URI, and any parameters we want to provide to the endpoint. Afterwards, the `ring.mock.request` function runs that request map through our stack, executing everything along the matching route handler.

In that spirit, we can test and ensure that our `/signup` POST route, will not return a 302 redirect to the `/signup-success` GET route unless all of the parameters (`:email`, `:username`, and `:password`) are valid. We'll construct another test context, and create the first assertion—that a missing e-mail returns a 200 response OK instead of a 302 redirect. Use following lines of code to do this:

```
(deftest missing-email-address-redisplays-the-form
  (let [response (app (request :post "/signup"
    {:username "TheDude" :password "123456789"}))]
    (is (= 200 (:status response)))))
```

This test will actually invoke our `/signup` POST route in our `home-routes`, and drill all the way through the plumbing, including rendering the response. Note that integration tests will also interact with any external, dependent systems, such as the database. As such, it's important that you pay pay close attention to what your integration test interacts with; if it mutates any data, you must reset that data prior to running the next test. For this reason, we will not test for a successful 302 redirect because this would ultimately pollute our database.

Unit testing is an academic pursuit well beyond the means of this book. If you are interested in getting deep into unit testing, I highly recommend that you read Gerard Meszaros' *xUnit Test Patterns*, a book with an incredible wealth of knowledge when it comes to writing sustainable automated tests.

# Summary

That's about as quick of a whirlwind tour as one can get when it comes to testing. You learned the basics of how to write unit and integration tests, as well as some decent high-level guidance about what we should and should not test. In the next chapter, we'll finally start looking at how we can interact with the database so we can finally create the user account.

# 7
# Getting Started with the Database

In my first year of computer science education, I tried to avoid databases as much as possible. I naively said, "Why do I need to learn about databases? I have no desire to be a DBA!" It didn't take long until I realized you can't do anything interesting and ongoing if you don't know how to interact with a database. So far, we've created a fair bit of plumbing in our hipstr application, but we have yet to actually save anything to the database. This chapter is going to change all of this. In this chapter, we will cover the following topics:

* Set up the database schema using **PostgreSQL**
* Learn how to maintain and migrate database schemas using the Migratus Leiningen plugin
* Insert data from the Sign Up form (built in *Chapter 5*, *Handling Form Input*) into the database using the brilliantly simple SQL library **YeSQL**

This, and the following three chapters, will cover basic database interactions. This chapter provides the foundation of the meat of our application. I hope you're hungry.

# Creating the database schema

Before we interact with a database, we'll need to actually create a database schema, go figure, as you can't harvest eggs without the chicken. In this section, we're going set up the database schema for our hipstr application, using PostgreSQL.

> This section assumes you already have the PostgreSQL database server installed on your machine, and thus, will not guide you through that process. You can download PostgreSQL at `http://www.postgresql.org/download/`. This book was written using PostgreSQL 9.3.5 OS X application on Mac OS X Yosemite.

You may be asking, "Why a database schema instead of a new database?" You can do either, really. The advantage of creating a new database schema over a database, however, comes in the form of role and user management, which for the most part, we won't get into except to create the user for the hipstr application. Let's do this now.

Perform the following steps as either a super user (if you already have a PostgreSQL super user set up) or the default postgres user. This example will use the built-in postgres user:

1.  From the terminal, launch psql:

    ```
    # psql -U postgres -d postgres -h localhost
    ```

    The preceding command basically says, "Hey, launch psql as the Postgresql user (-U) postgres, connect to the database (-d) postgres, on the host (-h) localhost."

> Note that how you installed PostgreSQL will determine how you launch the `psql` tool. In this chapter, we will use the preceding command, however, your setup might be different. For example, you might need to use `sudo`:
>
> ```
> # sudo su -- postgres; psql
> ```
>
> If you installed the PostgreSQL app for OS X, you can launch `psql` by choosing the `Open psql` option from the PostgreSQL menu item. However, all instructions involving `psql` assume we're connecting to the default PostgreSQL database. To use `psql` and connect to the `postgres` database, do the following:
> ```
> # /Applications/Postgres.app/Contents/
> Versions/9.3/bin/psql -d postgres
> ```

2.  Create the hipstr database role and give it the ability to connect to the database as though it were a user:

```
postgres=# CREATE ROLE hipstr LOGIN;
```

3.  We should give the new hipstr role a password. Something really secure, like p455w0rd. We can do this using the \password command.

```
postgres=# \password hipstr;
```

4.  Now that we have a role, with which we can use to log in to the database, we should create the hipstr schema and assign our hipstr role to be a pompous overlord of that schema:

```
postgres=# CREATE SCHEMA AUTHORIZATION hipstr;
postgres=# GRANT ALL ON SCHEMA hipstr TO hipstr;
postgres=# GRANT ALL ON ALL TABLES IN SCHEMA hipstr TO hipstr;
```

The first line in the preceding code is shorthand for saying, "Hey, create me a schema for the user hipstr, and also give that schema a name of hipstr." In the next line, we grant all permissions in the hipstr schema to our hipstr role, and finally we give the hipstr role dominion over all the tables in the hipstr schema.

 Yes, in the real world, this method isn't exactly the most secure but it's not entirely terrible either. You can always partition access to your database using different roles with different permissions and whatnot, but that's an overkill for our little application. In reality, your cloud provider, hosting provider, database administrator, or somebody will likely give you a more secure user than what we're creating here.

5.  We can limit the scope of what the hipstr role sees by defining its search path. We can do this by doing the following:

```
postgres=# ALTER USER hipstr SET search_path = 'hipstr';
```

6.  Finally, exit the PostgreSQL shell.

```
postgres=# \q
```

Assuming all the preceding commands are executed without error, the whole process should look something like the following:

```
● ● ●                    ⌂ ryanbaldwin — bash — Solarized Dark ansi — 80×21
                                           bash                                            +
Last login: Mon Dec  1 18:41:11 on ttys001
bigfoot:~ ryanbaldwin$ '/Applications/Postgres.app/Contents/Versions/9.3/bin'/p
sql -p5432
psql (9.3.5)
Type "help" for help.

ryanbaldwin=# CREATE ROLE hipstr LOGIN;
CREATE ROLE
ryanbaldwin=# \password hipstr;
Enter new password:
Enter it again:
ryanbaldwin=# CREATE SCHEMA AUTHORIZATION hipstr;
CREATE SCHEMA
ryanbaldwin=# GRANT ALL ON SCHEMA hipstr TO hipstr;
GRANT
ryanbaldwin=# GRANT ALL ON ALL TABLES IN SCHEMA hipstr TO hipstr;
GRANT
ryanbaldwin=# ALTER USER hipstr SET search_path = 'hipstr';
ALTER ROLE
ryanbaldwin=# \q
bigfoot:~ ryanbaldwin$ █
```

After disconnecting from the PostgreSQL shell, we can test out our new user by logging in to the default database using the hipstr role.

Back at the terminal, relaunch psql, but this time using the hisptr role we created:

```
# psql -U hipstr -d postgres -h localhost
```

You might be asking, "Why are we still connecting to the "postgres" database?" Remember, in step 4, we didn't create a new database, rather, we created a new schema in the "postgres" database.

You should be able to successfully connect to the postgres database using your hipstr user. If you receive an error message about how the hipstr user cannot login, ensure that you included LOGIN in step 2.

Next, we can issue a couple of psql commands, \conninfo and \dn to ensure that we're all set up. The following is the output of those two commands:

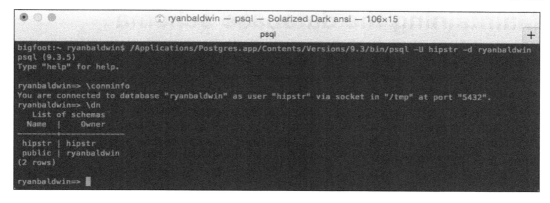

The \conninfo and \dn commands perform the following actions:

- \conninfo: This lists which database we are connecting to, on which port, and under which user

- \dn: This displays a list of schemas and who owns each of those schemas

If what you see on your own screen is what we see in the preceding screenshots, then we should be ready to rock with the rest of this chapter.

 If you're still having problems connecting, you may need to adjust the host-based authentication in the pg_hba.conf file to allow for local connections. The pg_hba.conf file itself has decent documentation. A gist of what you'll be looking to adjust is at the bottom of the file where various authentication schemes are defined (socket connections, IPv4 local connections, and so on). My pg_hba.conf file for the default database is located in /opt/local/var/db/postgresql93/defaultdb/pg_hba.conf, though your mileage may vary.

Finally, the last thing we need to do is to add the PostgreSQL JDBC driver to our application. Add the following dependency to your project.clj file's :dependencies vector:

```
[postgresql/postgresql "9.3-1102.jdbc41"]
```

 Note that your version of the postgresql driver may be different if you did not install Version 9.3 of PostgreSQL.

# Maintaining the database schema

A pain point common in nearly every team-based project I've ever worked on is how to manage the database. More often than not, teams decide to have a central *development* database, and all the developers use that central development database as their backing DB while making changes. This invariably results in somebody breaking somebody else's application under development because the database schema gets changed in some way, or test data gets removed or modified, and so on. Having a single monolithic development database can be real nasty, and is something that I try to avoid.

I'm a firm believer that a developer should be able to check out the source code, and within a few keystrokes, be able to successfully build and run the application. This is difficult, if not impossible, to do without having some kind of automated tool to build a database on the developer's own local machine. Thankfully, some kind souls on the Internet share my ideals and have created various tools to try and help with this whole thing. One of the better Leiningen plugins that I've used to accomplish this is **Migratus**.

# Migratus

Migratus is an API and plugin for Leiningen that automatically migrates, and rolls back, our database. In a nutshell, it allows us to create a series of SQL scripts, which will be executed in order (based on filename) against our database. We can migrate a defined set of scripts, or all scripts. Conversely, we can roll back a defined set of scripts (however, there does not exist an option to rollback the whole lot).

The beauty of Migratus is we can commit our SQL files in version control and other developers will receive them when they perform an update (or if we get a new machine, or want to sync between a desktop and laptop, and the like). All they have to do to migrate their database after a `git pull` command, for example, is run `lein migratus` from their project root. Migratus will then run any migration files against a target database that have not yet been run. Done.

The remainder of this book will use Migratus to manage our database schema changes. As such, it might be useful to know how to actually get it.

 You can view the full documentation for Migratus at `https://github.com/pjstadig/migratus`.

# Getting Migratus

Migratus comes in two forms: an API (which is useful for having migration scripts run as part of a start-up process if you're deploying) and a plugin for Leiningen.

To get the API, add it to the list of `:dependencies` in your project.clj file:

```
[migratus "0.7.0"]
```

To get the Leiningen plugin (which we will be using), add the following code to the list of `:plugins` in the hipstr `project.clj` file:

```
[migratus-lein "0.1.0"]
```

Running a simple `lein deps` command from the command line will download the new dependencies.

# Configuring Migratus

Now that we've added the Migratus plugin, we also need to configure it. After all, Migratus is not magical; it doesn't *just work* without a bit of guidance. Migratus' configuration, like most configurations, is thrown in hipstr's `project.clj` file under the keyword `:migratus`. The configuration contains three key pieces of information: what we're migrating (the `:store` — in our case, a database), where the migration scripts are kept (`:migration-dir`), and any configuration settings for the store in question. Add the following code to the hipstr `project.clj` file:

```
; ...
:migratus {
  :store              :database
  :migration-dir "migrations"
  :migration-table-name "_migrations"
  :db              {:classname    "org.postgresql.Driver"
    :subprotocol "postgresql"
    :subname     "//localhost/postgres"
    :user        "hipstr"
    :password    "p455w0rd"}}
; ...
```

Let's take a look at the Migratus configuration keys from the preceding code:

*   `:store`: This defines the target object we are migrating. In our case, we're migrating a database, so we use the `:database` key. Supposedly, Migratus is a generic migrations library, but I've not seen it officially support anything other than databases.

- :migration-dir: This defines the directory on the classpath where our SQL migration scripts are stored. We'll create a directory called migrations under our src directory.

- :migration-table-name: This is an optional configuration key, but useful when using schemas instead of standalone databases. Migratus uses an underlying table to track which migrations have been run and which have not. We can specify the name of this table. This table name defaults to schema_migrations, however I've found that it can, for whatever reason, be somewhat buggy when using schemas.

- :db: The meat of the configuration, this tells the Migratus plugin how to connect to the database. The value map in our configuration should look familiar, as it leverages what we've done in the preceding sections of this chapter.

 You'll need to modify the :db :subname value to point to the appropriate database, if you have not created the hipstr schema in the default postgres database. In OS X, for example, my default database is //localhost/ryanbaldwin.

We can test this configuration by running the Migratus plugin. Type the following in your terminal from the root of your hipstr directory:

```
# lein migratus migrate
```

This will migrate any yet-to-be-run migration script inside our migrations directory, and emit information about the status of each migration. In our case, because we haven't written any migrations yet, we should see something similar to the following:

```
hipstr — bash — Solarized Dark ansi — 69×12
                              bash                              +
bigfoot:~ ryanbaldwin$ cd ~/dev/hipstr/
bigfoot:hipstr ryanbaldwin$ lein migratus migrate
Dec 01, 2014 7:31:51 PM clojure.tools.logging$eval289$fn__293 invoke
INFO: creating migration table '_migrations'
Dec 01, 2014 7:31:51 PM clojure.tools.logging$eval289$fn__293 invoke
INFO: Starting migrations
Beginning migrations
No migrations found
Dec 01, 2014 7:31:52 PM clojure.tools.logging$eval289$fn__293 invoke
INFO: Ending migrations
Migrations complete
bigfoot:hipstr ryanbaldwin$ 
```

In the preceding output, we can see that Migratus created the `_migrations` table we configured to keep track of migrations. We're informed that no migrations were found. Let's fix this!

# Creating the user table

To create the database tables for our hipstr application, we'll write good old fashioned SQL scripts. For each table, we'll create an `up` script, which Migratus executes while migrating our database, and a `down` script, which Migratus executes when rolling back.

 Migratus is very particular about the naming of scripts. It expects a 14-digit number as the script's prefix, paired with any combination of characters, and finally suffixed with a `.up.sql` or `.down.sql`, respectively. The rational for this design decision was so that each migration script would have a date/time prefix, which supposedly helps in a distributed version control system such as Git, where multiple branches and such may exist. In our case, however, that's overkill, so we'll just use incremental version numbers.

Create a migrations directory at `src/migrations`. Next, create your first Migratus script, and call it `00000000000100-users.up.sql`, and save it in the `src/migrations` directory (all subsequent Migratus scripts that we write will go in this directory).

The content of the Migratus script is just SQL. We'll create a simple user table that captures the data from our signup form, along with a couple of timestamps. Add the following SQL to the `users.up.sql` script:

```
CREATE TABLE users
(user_id     SERIAL      NOT NULL PRIMARY KEY,
 username    VARCHAR(30) NOT NULL,
 email       VARCHAR(60),
 password    VARCHAR(100),
 created_at TIMESTAMP    NOT NULL DEFAULT (now() AT TIME ZONE
 'utc'),
 updated_at TIMESTAMP    NOT NULL DEFAULT (now() AT TIME ZONE
 'utc'));
--;;
-- create a function which simply sets the update_date column to the
-- current date/time.

CREATE OR REPLACE FUNCTION update_updated_at()
RETURNS TRIGGER AS $$
BEGIN
```

```
    NEW.updated_at = now() AT TIME ZONE 'utc';
    RETURN NEW;
END
$$ language 'plpgsql';
--;;
-- create an update trigger which updates our updated_at column by
-- calling the above function
CREATE TRIGGER update_user_updated_at BEFORE UPDATE
ON users FOR EACH ROW EXECUTE PROCEDURE
update_updated_at();
```

There are three statements in this script, each of which are separated using the special --;; delimiter, which Migratus uses to split statements. The first statement creates the users table; the second statement creates a function responsible for keeping the updated_at column current; the third statement creates a BEFORE UPDATE trigger to ensure that the current date is set on the update_at column.

We can test the script by heading back over to our terminal and executing another lein migratus migrate command. You should see output similar to the following screenshot:

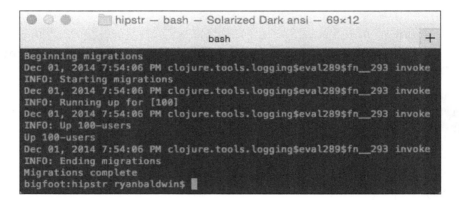

By all accounts, the migration appears to have completed successfully. Let's fire up the PostgreSQL management shell again and take a look at what was created.

From the terminal, launch the psql tool the same way we did earlier in this chapter in the Creating the Database Schema section:

**# psql -U hipstr -d postgres -h localhost**

Type the command \dt, which lists all the tables in the current schema:

**postgres=> \dt**

You should see something like the following:

```
● ○ ●                    hipstr — psql — Solarized Dark ansi — 121×13
                                          psql                                              +
bigfoot:hipstr ryanbaldwin$ '/Applications/Postgres.app/Contents/Versions/9.3/bin'/psql -p5432 -U hipstr -d ryanbaldwin
psql (9.3.5)
Type "help" for help.

ryanbaldwin=> \dt
              List of relations
 Schema |    Name     | Type  | Owner
--------+-------------+-------+--------
 hipstr | _migrations | table | hipstr
 hipstr | users       | table | hipstr
(2 rows)

ryanbaldwin=>
```

There you go! Our users table is in the hipstr schema! You can also issue a \d users command, to describe the table.

```
● ○ ●                    hipstr — psql — Solarized Dark ansi — 121×16
                                          psql                                              +
ryanbaldwin=> ryanbaldwin=> \d users
                               Table "hipstr.users"
   Column   |            Type             |                    Modifiers
------------+-----------------------------+----------------------------------------------------
 user_id    | integer                     | not null default nextval('users_user_id_seq'::regclass)
 username   | character varying(30)       | not null
 email      | character varying(60)       |
 password   | character varying(100)      |
 created_at | timestamp without time zone | not null default timezone('utc'::text, now())
 updated_at | timestamp without time zone | not null default timezone('utc'::text, now())
Indexes:
    "users_pkey" PRIMARY KEY, btree (user_id)
Triggers:
    update_user_updated_at BEFORE UPDATE ON users FOR EACH ROW EXECUTE PROCEDURE update_updated_at()

ryanbaldwin=>
```

# Dropping the user table

In the previous section, we created an up migration script. The up scripts are executed whenever we perform a lein migratus migrate or lein migratus up command. However, we should also create a down script, which is used when we want to roll back the database.

Create another migration script with the same name as the users.up script, but this time call it 00000000000100-users.down.sql. Migratus looks for the down portion of the filename when deciding which scripts to execute when rolling back, so don't forget this!

In the `users.up` script, we created a table, a function, and a trigger. In the `down` script, we'll want to remove these objects, but in the reverse order (lest we produce ill-fated SQL errors as a result of attempting to drop objects that are depended upon). This is achieved using the following code:

```
DROP TRIGGER update_user_updated_at ON users;
--;;
DROP FUNCTION update_updated_at();
--;;
DROP TABLE users;
```

The preceding code drops the three objects we created in the appropriate order.

# Running the down scripts

We can run the down scripts by running `lein migratus down` [list of migration script ids]. For example:

```
# lein migratus down 100
```

Migratus will attempt to execute each `down` script matching the list of IDs. Much like `lein migratus migrate`, Migratus will emit output informing us of the status of each rollback, similar to the following screenshot:

There currently does not exist an equivalent to Migratus' `lein migratus migrate` for running all `down` scripts, and thus we are forced to specify the ID of each down script we wish to execute. This is an unfortunate limitation, however Migratus is open source, so perhaps some generous Clojure whiz will be kind enough to write a `lein migratus down all` *cough*thanks*cough*.

# Migrating the database

Before we move forward and start actually interacting with the database from code, it would be worth considering how to migrate and roll back the database, both using Leiningen as well as programatically.

## Running all migration scripts from Leiningen

The commands to run migration scripts are as follows:

- `lein migratus migrate`: This runs all `up` migration scripts that are yet to be run. Migratus checks the migrations table, which consists of a single column of migration script IDs and runs any migrations that have not already been run (that is, any migration scripts whose ID is not already in the migrations table).

- `lein migratus up [IDs]`: This migrates one or more `up` migration scripts by specifying their ID. Each migration script is run in the order specified. If the migration script has already been run, it will be skipped.

  ```
  lein migratus up 100 200 300
  ```

- `lein migratus down [IDs]`: This runs the `down` script for each ID specified, in the order of the IDs specified, for example:

  ```
  lein migratus down 300 200 100
  ```

## Running migrations programatically

This is quite possibly one of my favorite features of Migratus. I've spent far too many late nights deploying software, and botching SQL scripts. I'm a fan of single-click deployment or, at the very least, minimizing the amount of effort it takes to get a piece of software deployed. One of the things I like to do—either because I'm clever or stupid—is to tap into the Migratus API at startup (such as in the `hipstr.handler/init`) and run any migration that may be required. This frees up our effort when deploying our app for the first time, or on subsequent upgrades. As long as we have the proper database connection, the app will take care of the rest.

The Migratus API follows the same options as its Leiningen plugin counterpart, and has the following functions:

- `migratus.core/migrate`: This runs all `up` migration scripts that are yet to be run.

- `migratus.core/up [IDs]`: This migrates one or more `up` scripts by specifying their ID, in the defined order. Again, this skips any `up` script that's already been run.

- `migratus.core/down [IDs]`: This runs one or more `down` scripts by specifying their ID, in the defined order.

That's it—a tiny API that can make the deployment story a lot easier. For fun, let's add automatic migrations in our `hipstr.handler` namespace.

## Adding migrations to the hipstr initialization

Adding migrations to the hisptr application is easy. We can have Migratus run any required migrations upon application startup by adding the appropriate call in our `hipstr.handler/init` location. Let's do it now:

1. Add a Migratus config to our `hipstr.handler` namespace (we will refactor this later, I promise). For now, just copy and paste the `:migratus` value from the `project.clj` file:

```
(def migratus-config
  {:store :database
   :migration-dir "migrations"
   :migration-table-name "_migrations"
   :db {:classname "org.postgresql.Driver"
        :subprotocol "postgresql"
        :subname "//localhost/postgres"
        :user "hipstr"
        :password "p455w0rd"}})
```

2. Next, add the function that will perform the actual migration using `migratus.core/migrate`, marked as #1. We'll wrap it in a try/catch function and emit any errors in case the migration fails:

```
(defn migrate-db []
  (timbre/info "checking migrations")
  (try
    (migratus.core/migrate migratus-config) ;#1
    (catch Exception e
      (timbre/error "Failed to migrate" e)))
  (timbre/info "finished migrations"))
```

3. Lastly, add a call to `migrate-db` in the `hipstr.handler/init` function, right before we call `session-manager/cleanup-job`:

```
;...snipped for brevity
(migrate-db)
(cronj/start! session-manager/cleanup-job)
```

That's it! Now start the app with a `lein ring server` command (or restart it if you already have it running) and watch the output. You should see something similar to the following:

```
bigfoot:hipstr ryanbaldwin$ lein ring server
2014-Dec-02 20:49:17 -0500 bigfoot.local INFO [hipstr.handler] - checking migrations
Dec 02, 2014 8:49:18 PM clojure.tools.logging$eval8040$fn__8044 invoke
INFO: Starting migrations
Dec 02, 2014 8:49:18 PM clojure.tools.logging$eval8040$fn__8044 invoke
INFO: Running up for [100]
Dec 02, 2014 8:49:18 PM clojure.tools.logging$eval8040$fn__8044 invoke
INFO: Up 100-users
Dec 02, 2014 8:49:18 PM clojure.tools.logging$eval8040$fn__8044 invoke
INFO: Ending migrations
2014-Dec-02 20:49:18 -0500 bigfoot.local INFO [hipstr.handler] - finished migrations
2014-Dec-02 20:49:18 -0500 bigfoot.local INFO [hipstr.handler] -
-=[ hipstr started successfully using the development profile ]=-
2014-12-02 20:49:18.600:INFO:oejs.Server:jetty-7.6.13.v20130916
2014-12-02 20:49:18.622:INFO:oejs.AbstractConnector:Started SelectChannelConnector@0.0.0.0:3000
Started server on port 3000
```

In the preceding image, you can see that Migratus ran any required migrations as part of the hipstr initialization.

# Adding data to the database

There are a thousand and one ways to get data into, and out of, a database. I confess that I am not a fan of ORMs such as Hibernate because over the long term, I think they're far more costly than writing your own SQL. ORMs are convenient during development, and they keep the code consistent, but they abstract SQL so far away that it can be difficult to diagnose what's happening when your data access isn't performing how you expect it to (whether it be performance, incorrect data retrieval, or something more sinister). Of course, ORMs have their value in the sense that they're (mostly) database agnostic, but never once in my career have I worked on anything wherein the backend database was a variable.

This being said, I also loath SQL strings in my code. They're ugly, they're hard to read, they remove much of the built-in SQL highlighting and support of many modern IDEs, they force you to create weird classes with nothing but SQL templates in them, and they just feel wrong.

For the most part, those two options have been our only options: either write your own SQL inside your Java/Clojure/C#/Python/Whatever code, or have some library mysteriously generate it for you. The risk/reward is six of one and a half dozen of the other.

It's for these reasons why I was so strongly attracted to YeSQL.

# What is YeSQL?

YeSQL is a tiny Clojure library, which generates functions out of your own SQL. That's right. You write your own SQL code in a separate .sql file, and at runtime YeSQL pulls it in and turns it into a function. You then call that function, passing it an argument map, and voila! Data!

This allows you to keep your SQL separate from the rest of your Clojure code, but more importantly, it allows you to treat your SQL as SQL.

For example, pretend we have the following query in a file called foobars.sql:

```
SELECT *
FROM foo
WHERE
  severity = 'BAR'
```

YeSQL can pull this query in and wrap it in a Clojure function in two brain dead steps:

1.  Annotate the query with a name and optional doc string:

    ```
    -- name: get-foobars
    -- Gets all the really bad foos. All of them.
    SELECT *
    FROM foo
    WHERE
      severity='BAR'
    ```

2.  In your namespace, slurp in the SQL file:

    ```
    (require '[yesql.core :refer [defqueries])
    (defqueries "foobars.sql" [some database connection stuff])
    ```

That's it. Now our namespace will have access to a function that matches the name annotation we set on the query, in our case, get-foobars. We call that query the same way we call any other function in Clojure. Not only this, but any extra documentation we added to the query also gets pulled in as a docstring. Nifty!

The rest of this book will use YeSQL for all interactions with the database.

 You can find the docs for YeSQL 0.5.0-beta2 at https://github. com/krisajenkins/yesql/tree/v0.5.0-beta2.

# Getting YeSQL

As with everything else Leiningen based, grabbing the YeSQL library is a one-step process. In our `project.clj`, add the following to the `:dependencies` list:

```
[yesql "0.5.0-beta2"]
```

That's all we have to do. There is no additional configuration or setup.

YeSQL 0.5.0-beta2 is a bit of a departure from 0.4.0, and is not backwards compatible. YeSQL 0.4.0 used positional arguments for all the generated functions, which were difficult to maintain after the fact (think about insert statements! Craziness!). 0.5.x does away with positional arguments and uses map arguments. This makes the code much cleaner and easier to use. We will be using YeSQL 0.5.x because, with luck, it will be stable by the time this book comes to light.

# Adding a user to the database

The easiest way to get started with YeSQL is for us to complete our User Signup form. To get started, do the following:

1. Create a new directory, `src/hipstr/models`, where we'll put our `.sql` files and other database like code.

2. Create a new SQL file in the `models` directory called `users.sql`. This is where we will put our SQL for inserting and getting a user.

Create a new Clojure file alongside `users.sql`, called `user_model.clj`. This will be a (very) thin wrapper around the YeSQL generated query functions.

## Inserting a user using SQL

Our users table is a simple one, which only requires three values from us at the time of inserting: username, email, and password (the others, `created_at`, `updated_at`, and `user_id` are autogenerated for us). As such, the SQL is straight forward. Open the `users.sql` file and enter the following:

```
-- name: insert-user<!
-- Inserts a new user into the Users table
-- Expects :username, :email, and :password
INSERT INTO users (username, email, password)
VALUES (:username, :email, :password)
```

The preceding code looks pretty standard. We're inserting a new row into the users table, and are providing each the username, email, and password columns a value. In the VALUES clause, we are specifying a :username, :email, and :password key, each of which will be bound to the map passed to the generated function.

SQL aside, we also used the name: annotation, which YeSQL uses for the name of the generated function, and a docstring, which YeSQL also uses to document the generated function. However, there's another interesting syntax, and that's the < ! suffix we gave the name.

There are two special suffixes we can use in the names of our YeSQL queries. These suffixes tell YeSQL to return an appropriate result when mutable queries (that is, queries that insert/update/delete/alter the database) are executed. These suffixes are as follows:

- < !: Query names ending in < ! will return either the primary key, or the entire altered row, depending on the database driver. Using PostgreSQL, the entire row will be returned. Take a look at the following example:

```
(insert-user<! {:username "TheDude"
                :email "thedude@bides.net"
                :password "abc123"})
=> {:update_date #inst "2014-09-27T19:02:25.206296000-
00:00"
    :create_date #inst "2014-09-27T19:02:25.206296000-
00:00"
    :pass "abc123" :email "thedude@bides.net"
    :username "TheDude", :user_id 13}
```

- !: Query names ending in ! will return the number of rows affected by the query. For example, if we changed our insert-user<! to just insert-user!, our code would produce the following:

```
(insert-user! {:username "TheDude"
               :email "thedude@bides.net"
               :password "abc123"})
=> 1
```

These two special characters are convenient when we want to report appropriate outcomes to the client.

# Inserting a user using Clojure

Now that we have the SQL file with the insert statement, we need to give our `user_model.clj` file some meat. Open up the `user_model.clj` file and add the following code:

```clojure
(ns hipstr.models.user-model
  (:require [yesql.core :refer [defqueries]]))

(def db-spec {:classname "org.postgresql.Driver"  ;#1
              :subprotocol "postgresql"
              :subname   "//localhost/postgres"
              :user      "hipstr"
              :password  "p455w0rd"})

(defqueries "hipstr/models/users.sql"
            {:connection db-spec})    ; #2
```

The preceding code is all we need for YeSQL to generate a series of functions out of all the SQL we write in the `users.sql` file. At #1 we are defining our database connection. This should look pretty familiar to the JDBC connection maps that one provides when using vanilla `clojure.jdbc` (which is what YeSQL uses under the hood—there's no magic there).

Code at #2 is, however, where the magic happens. At #2 we tell YeSQL," *Hey*, go look at the `users.sql` file and generate a function for each query, and for each query use this database connection." In essence, our SQL becomes our data model, and the `user_model` namespace is a thin shim connecting our business to the data model.

Passing the connection to `defqueries` is a convenience and not necessary. If we left it out, however, we would have to provide the connection anytime we called the generated function, for example `(insert-user<! {:username...} {db-spec})`. This gets annoying, and it creates unnecessary clutter in our code.

 The database connection doesn't have to be defined as part of the `user_model` namespace, and indeed, it shouldn't, as all our models will connect to the same database. We will refactor this as part of *Chapter 11, Environment Configurations and Deployment.*

We can do a sanity check using the REPL to ensure that the preceding code actually works:

```
# lein repl
hipstr.repl=> (load "models/user_model")
hipstr.repl=> (ns hipstr.models.user-model)
```

```
hipstr.repl=> (:doc (meta insert-user<!))
>> "Inserts a new user into the Users table\nExpects :username,
:email, and :password"
hipstr.repl=> (insert-user<! {:username "test" :email "test@foo.bar"
:password "abc123"})
>> {:updated_at #inst "2014-12-03T07:48:53...." :created_at #inst
"2014-12-03T07:48:53..." :password "abc123" :email "test@foo.bar"
:username "test" :user_id 1}
```

With the knowledge that it works, we can complete our Signup process.

# Bringing it all together

So far, we've created a users table, a SQL query for inserting a user record, and a thin shim that generates Clojure functions from our SQL queries. It's time we bring these into our Signup workflow and get the user in the database.

## Adjusting the route

As it stands, the only thing we actually have to do is adjust our /signup POST route. Open the hipstr.routes.home namespace and perform the following steps:

1.  Adjust the :require form to make use of our new user-model namespace:

    ```
    (:require [compojure.core :refer :all]

        ...

        [hipstr.models.user-model :as u]))
    ```

2.  Adjust our signup-page-submit function such that we'll add the new user to the database if all validations pass:

    ```
    (defn signup-page-submit [user]
      (let [errors (v/validate-signup user)]
        (if (empty? errors)
          (do
            (u/insert-user<! user)
            (response/redirect "/signup-success"))
          (layout/render "signup.html"
                         (assoc user :errors errors)))))
    ```

That's all we need to do. We simply pass our user map to the function generated by YeSQL and our newly signed-up user is saved to the database. This works because our user form's field names map perfectly to the keys expected by the generated insert-user<! function. However, there is one more thing we'll want to do with our data before we save it.

# Encrypting the password

We are good developers. We care (somewhat) about security (I hope). As such, we'll want to encrypt the password before we store it in the database. This is not something we want to worry about every time we add a new user, so we'll add a small function in our `hipstr.models.user-model` namespace, which will encrypt the password before we throw it in the database.

The easiest way to encrypt a password is to use crypto-password, a tiny encryption library written by James Reeves (yep, him again). To encrypt our user's password, do the following:

1.  Add the `crypto-password` dependency by adding the following code to our `project.clj` dependencies:

    ```
    [crypto-password "0.1.3"]
    ```

2.  Add `crypto-password` as a requirement in our `hisptr.models.user-model` namespace. The `crypto-password` lib supports 3 encryption schemes: PBKDF2, bcrypt, and scrypt. For the purpose of this exercise ,we will use bcrypt:

    ```
    (ns hipstr.models.user-model
      (:require [yesql.core :refer [defqueries]]
        [crypto.password.bcrypt :as password]))
    ```

3.  Create a small function, `add-user!`, which our `/signup` POST route will call. This function will simply encrypt the `:password` key on the incoming user map before passing it off to the `insert-user<!` function generated by YeSQL.

    ```
    (defn add-user!
      "Saves a user to the database."
      [user]
      (let [new-user (->> (password/encrypt (:password user))
                          (assoc user :password)
                          insert-user<!)]
                          (dissoc new-user :pass)))
    ```

4.  Finally, adjust the `/signup` POST route back in our `hipstr.routes.home` namespace to use the new `hipstr.models.user-model/add-user!` function instead of directly calling the `insert-user<!` function:

    ```
    ...
    (do
      (u/add-user! user)
      (response/redirect "/signup-success"))))
    ```

We are now storing a fully encrypted password in our database, and we barely had to do a thing. Go ahead and restart hipstr, and start accepting billions of users.

# Summary

We came a long way in this chapter. We shared a few laughs, and we learned some valuable life lessons along the way. You learned how you can sanely manage your database schema using Migratus, as well as how you can use SQL without cluttering your Clojure code using YeSQL. The Migratus/YeSQL combination allows you to quickly develop and maintain your database without giving up the power, flexibility, and visibility of raw SQL, something we typically sacrifice when using an ORM. In the next chapter, we'll continue using YeSQL as we create the login form for our application.

# 8
# Reading Data from the Database

In *Chapter 7*, *Getting Started with the Database*, we covered a lot of ground: We created a database schema and granted our application access, we were introduced to Migratus and started using it to create our first table, and we were introduced to YeSQL for inserting data into the DB without the use of any ORM sorcery. In this chapter, we will continue our example by fetching data from the database. We will be:

- Creating two new tables: albums and artists
- Seeding our new tables with example data
- Creating a new page that displays the recently added albums
- Creating a new artist page
- Linking the *Recently Added* page to the artist page

Much of this chapter should appear obvious after everything we've done so far. So let's get to work!

## Creating the catalog

At this point, we want to lay the foundation of allowing our user to catalog and view their record collection. We will create a simple *Recently Added* album page, and a simple *Show me all the albums for this artist* page (which I'll just call "the artist page"). The first thing to do in order to facilitate this incredible functionality is to create the artists table and the albums table.

# Creating the artists table

We will use Migratus to create the artists table. As such, we need to create another SQL migration file. So let's do the following:

1. In the `src/migrations` folder, create a new migration script called `00000000000200-artists.up.sql`.

2. For our hipstr app, the artists table is going to be extremely simple. We'll have an `artist_id` that uniquely identifies the artist, a `name` (go figure), and two timestamps, `created_at` and `updated_at`, for keeping track of when the artist was created and last updated. Add the following SQL:

```
CREATE TABLE artists                                    -- #1
( artist_id SERIAL NOT NULL PRIMARY KEY,
  name VARCHAR(255) NOT NULL,
  created_at TIMESTAMP NOT NULL DEFAULT (now() AT TIME ZONE
  'utc'),
  updated_at TIMESTAMP NOT NULL DEFAULT (now() AT TIME ZONE 'utc'),
  CONSTRAINT artist_name UNIQUE(name));
--;;
-- create an update trigger which updates our updated_at
-- column by calling the above function
CREATE TRIGGER update_artist_updated_at BEFORE UPDATE   --#2
ON artists FOR EACH ROW EXECUTE PROCEDURE
update_updated_at();
```

In the artists migrations script, we wrote a CREATE TABLE statement (#1), which should look familiar (it's very similar to our users table). Similar to the user's table, we put a BEFORE UPDATE trigger (#2), which allows our database to manage the updated_at field and not rely on us to maintain it every time we update the record. The update_updated_at function is created as part of the `00000000000100-users.up.sql` migration.

We can ensure that the previous script works by first using Migratus, and then use psql to ensure that the table was created. Do the following:

1. From the command line, migrate the database to include the artists table by using migratus:

   ```
   # lein migratus migrate
   ```

2. Connect to the database using the psql tool:

   ```
   # psql -U hipstr -d postgres -h localhost
   ```

3. Use the `\dt` command to list all the tables available to the current role:

   ```
   postgres=> \dt
   ```

If everything succeeds as it should, you will see something similar to the following:

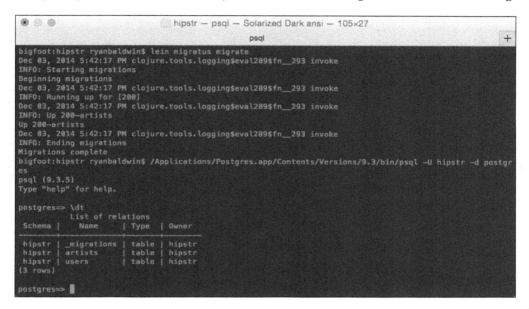

Of course, we can't have an up migration without a down migration, as that's just not going to fly when we're developing and we want to reset the universe. So let's create the down migration for the artists table by doing the following:

1.  In the src/migrations folder, create a new migration script called 00000000000200-artists.down.sql.

2.  Write an SQL statement that destroys the artists table:

    ```
    DROP TABLE artists;
    ```

(Again, we can ensure that our script works by rolling back just the artists table using lein migratus down, and then psql'ing to the database and running the same \dt command):

1.  From the command line, roll back the artists table:

    ```
    # lein migratus down 200
    ```

2.  Connect to the database using psql:

    ```
    # psql -U hipstr -d localhost -h localhost
    ```

3.  Use the psql command to list all the tables, which will magically no longer list our artists table:

    ```
    postgres=> \dt
    ```

Again, if everything succeeds, we will see something similar to the following:

```
bigfoot:hipstr ryanbaldwin$ lein migratus down 200
Dec 03, 2014 5:51:58 PM clojure.tools.logging$eval289$fn__293 invoke
INFO: Starting migrations
Beginning migrations
Dec 03, 2014 5:51:58 PM clojure.tools.logging$eval289$fn__293 invoke
INFO: Running down for [200]
Dec 03, 2014 5:51:58 PM clojure.tools.logging$eval289$fn__293 invoke
INFO: Down 200-artists
Down 200-artists
Dec 03, 2014 5:51:58 PM clojure.tools.logging$eval289$fn__293 invoke
INFO: Ending migrations
Migrations complete
bigfoot:hipstr ryanbaldwin$ /Applications/Postgres.app/Contents/Versions/9.3/bin/psql -U hipstr -d postg
res
psql (9.3.5)
Type "help" for help.

postgres=> \dt
          List of relations
 Schema |    Name    | Type  | Owner
--------+------------+-------+--------
 hipstr | _migrations | table | hipstr
 hipstr | users      | table | hipstr
(2 rows)

postgres=>
```

However, since this chapter is mostly focusing on reading data and not adding data (because I'm a crazy Canuck like that), we are going to need some data to work with.

# Seeding the artists table

Migratus is a *dumb* migration tool in that it doesn't know what it's executing; it just knows it's executing something. So there's nothing stopping us from seeding our artists table with data. This might seem like a weird thing to do. However, in a team environment – or even in your own development environment – this is a great way to easily seed the database. Let's add the following few insert statements to the bottom of our artists migration script so that we can seed it:

```
--;;
INSERT INTO artists (name) VALUES ('The Arthur Digby Sellers Band')
--;;
INSERT INTO artists (name) VALUES ('Fort Knox Harrington')
--;;
INSERT INTO artists (name) VALUES ('Hungus')
--;;
INSERT INTO artists (name) VALUES ('Smokey Fouler')
--;;
INSERT INTO artists (name) VALUES ('Brant')
```

All we need to create a new artist in our `artists` table at this point is the artist name, because all the other fields are calculated.

 Remember that we can have multiple statements in a migration file, so long as we separate each statement with a `--;;`. Also note that you can't have any blank lines between each statement, otherwise Migratus gets confused. And when Migratus gets confused, you'll get confused.

You can run `lein migratus migrate` to re-create the `artists` table and insert the seed data. If you'd like to ensure the table was properly seeded, you can use `psql` to run a query and ensure that the output is what we expect, as shown as follows:

```
● ● ●                    hipstr — psql — Solarized Dark ansi — 105×17
                                         psql                                              +
bigfoot:hipstr ryanbaldwin$ /Applications/Postgres.app/Contents/Versions/9.3/bin/psql -U hipstr -d postg
res
psql (9.3.5)
Type "help" for help.

postgres=> select * from artists;
 artist_id |            name             |         created_at         |         updated_at
-----------+-----------------------------+----------------------------+----------------------------
         1 | The Arthur Digby Sellers Band | 2014-12-03 22:57:07.470537 | 2014-12-03 22:57:07.470537
         2 | Fort Knox Harrington        | 2014-12-03 22:57:07.470537 | 2014-12-03 22:57:07.470537
         3 | Hungus                      | 2014-12-03 22:57:07.470537 | 2014-12-03 22:57:07.470537
         4 | Smokey Fouler               | 2014-12-03 22:57:07.470537 | 2014-12-03 22:57:07.470537
         5 | Brant                       | 2014-12-03 22:57:07.470537 | 2014-12-03 22:57:07.470537
(5 rows)

postgres=>
```

Now that we have the artists table up and running, it's time we create the `albums` table.

# Creating the albums table

For the sake of simplicity, this section will assume that an album can have a single artist. There's nothing stopping you from normalizing the database, such that you can create an `artists_albums` table that allows for a *many artists to many albums* approach. For this example, we'll assume a single album has a single artist, though an artist will have many albums.

As with `users` and `artists`, we will create `up` and `down` migration scripts. We'll be doing both of these as follows:

1. Create a new file in `src/migrations` location called `00000000000210-albums.up.sql`.

2. Add the following SQL to the albums migration file:

```sql
CREATE TABLE albums
(album_id      SERIAL      NOT NULL PRIMARY KEY,
 artist_id     BIGINT NOT NULL REFERENCES artists (artist_id),
 name          VARCHAR(255) NOT NULL,
 release_date DATE NOT NULL,
 created_at   TIMESTAMP    NOT NULL DEFAULT (now() AT TIME ZONE
'utc'),
 updated_at   TIMESTAMP    NOT NULL DEFAULT (now() AT TIME ZONE
'utc'),
 CONSTRAINT arist_album_name UNIQUE (artist_id, name));
--;;
-- create an update trigger which updates our update_date column
by calling the above function
CREATE TRIGGER update_album_updated_at BEFORE UPDATE
ON albums FOR EACH ROW EXECUTE PROCEDURE
update_updated_at();
--;;
INSERT INTO albums (artist_id, name, release_date)
  SELECT a.artist_id, 'My Iron Lung', '1978-11-24'
  FROM artists a
  WHERE a.name = 'The Arthur Digby Sellers Band'
--;;
INSERT INTO albums (artist_id, name, release_date)
  SELECT a.artist_id, 'American History Fail', '2000-04-18'
  FROM artists a
  WHERE a.name = 'The Arthur Digby Sellers Band'
--;;
INSERT INTO albums (artist_id, name, release_date)
  SELECT a.artist_id, 'Giggles and Mustaches', '1992-11-29'
  FROM artists a
  WHERE a.name = 'Fort Knox Harrington'
--;;
INSERT INTO albums (artist_id, name, release_date)
  SELECT a.artist_id, '20 Tons of Video Gold', '1990-10-09'
  FROM artists a
  WHERE a.name = 'Fort Knox Harrington'
--;;
INSERT INTO albums (artist_id, name, release_date)
  SELECT a.artist_id, 'Fixing the Cable', '1989-06-02'
  FROM artists a
  WHERE a.name = 'Hungus'
--;;
INSERT INTO albums (artist_id, name, release_date)
  SELECT a.artist_id, 'Over the Line', '1998-08-08'
```

```
        FROM artists a
        WHERE a.name = 'Smokey Fouler'
    --;;
    INSERT INTO albums (artist_id, name, release_date)
        SELECT a.artist_id, 'Petulant Suckup', '1995-05-21'
        FROM artists a
        WHERE a.name = 'Brant'
```

Similar to previous up migration scripts, we are creating a new table and employing the use of a BEFORE UPDATE trigger to manage the updated_at field.

We also seed the table with some example data using INSERT SELECT statements. INSERT SELECT statements allow us to populate the artist_id field without hardcoding the actual value of the artist_id field. Instead, we fetch the artist_id value just in time.

As with the artists table, we can create our albums table by running lein migratus migrate, and then use psql to verify that our albums table was properly created and seeded with data. You should see something similar to the screenshot shown as follows:

Also, let's not forget the down script. We can create it by following the same pattern as the `artists.down` script:

1. In the src/migrations folder, create a new migration script called `00000000000210-albums.down.sql`.

2. Write a SQL statement that destroys the albums table:

   ```
   DROP TABLE albums;
   ```

Ensure the script works by rolling back just the `albums` table using `lein migratus down`, and then `psql`'ing to the database and running the `\dt` command

1. From the command line, roll back the artists table:

   ```
   # lein migratus down 210
   ```

2. Connect to the database using `psql`:

   ```
   # psql -U hipstr -d localhost -h localhost
   ```

3. Use the `\dt` command to list all the tables that will no longer list the `albums` table:

   ```
   postgres=> \dt
   ```

If everything succeeds, you will see something similar to the following:

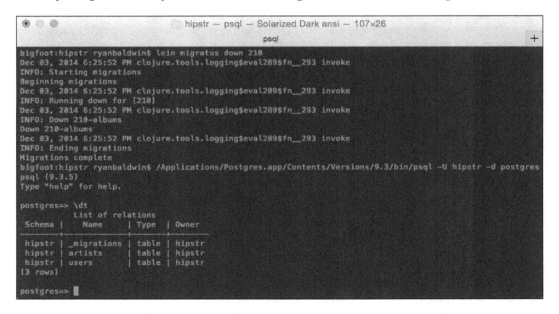

Before moving on, run `lein migratus migrate` to re-create and reseed the albums table, because now we're going to make use of it.

# Fetching albums from the database

In *Chapter 7, Getting Started with the Database*, we were introduced to YeSQL for interacting with our database. We used YeSQL to create an INSERT statement which added our new users to the database. Similarly, we can use YeSQL to SELECT records from the database. If you can do it in SQL, you can do it with YeSQL. And that's the beauty of YeSQL: it's just SQL. This allows us to open an SQL tool of our choice and experiment with our query until we get it right.

## Writing the SQL query

For this next bit, we'll use the psql tool to verify our SQL. But you're free to use whatever SQL editor you have at your disposal. Take the following steps:

1.  Launch psql and connect to our database:

    ```
    # psql -U hipstr -d postgres -h localhost
    ```

2.  We can write our query at the PostgreSQL prompt. Any valid SQL is accepted at the prompt; we just need to terminate it with a semi-colon (;). Our feature wants to show a list of albums, the artist/s, and the release dates of those albums, all ordered by the date on which it was added within hipstr. The corresponding query will look like the following:

    ```
    SELECT art.name as artist, alb.album_id, alb.name as album_name,
    alb.release_date, alb.created_at
    FROM artists art
    INNER JOIN albums alb ON art.artist_id = alb.artist_id
    ORDER BY alb.created_at DESC
    LIMIT 10;
    ```

Type the preceding script into the PostgreSQL prompt in `psql`. You should see something like the following:

```
● ● ●                    hipstr — psql — Solarized Dark ansi — 110×22
                                        psql                                                    +

bigfoot:hipstr ryanbaldwin$ /Applications/Postgres.app/Contents/Versions/9.3/bin/psql -U hipstr -d postgres
psql (9.3.5)
Type "help" for help.

postgres=> SELECT art.name as artist, alb.album_id, alb.name as album_name, alb.release_date, alb.created_at
postgres-> FROM artists art
postgres-> INNER JOIN albums alb ON art.artist_id = alb.artist_id
postgres-> ORDER BY alb.created_at DESC
postgres-> LIMIT 10;
            artist           | album_id |      album_name      | release_date |         created_at
-----------------------------+----------+----------------------+--------------+----------------------------
 The Arthur Digby Sellers Band |        2 | American History Fail | 2000-04-18   | 2014-12-03 23:32:05.141934
 The Arthur Digby Sellers Band |        1 | My Iron Lung          | 1978-11-24   | 2014-12-03 23:32:05.141934
 Fort Knox Harrington         |        4 | 20 Tons of Video Gold | 1990-10-09   | 2014-12-03 23:32:05.141934
 Fort Knox Harrington         |        3 | Giggles and Mustaches | 1992-11-29   | 2014-12-03 23:32:05.141934
 Hungus                       |        5 | Fixing the Cable      | 1989-06-02   | 2014-12-03 23:32:05.141934
 Smokey Fouler                |        6 | Over the Line         | 1998-08-08   | 2014-12-03 23:32:05.141934
 Brant                        |        7 | Petulant Suckup       | 1995-05-21   | 2014-12-03 23:32:05.141934
(7 rows)

postgres=> █
```

You can adjust and play with the query as you want in `psql`, but we'll use the one we wrote above.

Next, we'll create a new `albums.sql` file, where we'll define our YeSQL database function. We'll create this file alongside our existing `users.sql` file.

1. Create a new file in the `hipstr/models` directory and call it `albums.sql`.

2. Add the SQL we created in `psql`, and give it the name `get-recently-added` using the YeSQL naming annotation:

```
-- name: get-recently-added
-- Gets the 10 most recently added albums in the db.
SELECT art.name as artist, alb.album_id, alb.name as album_name,
alb.release_date, alb.created_at
FROM artists art
INNER JOIN albums alb ON art.artist_id = alb.artist_id
ORDER BY alb.created_at DESC
LIMIT 10;
```

That's it! As far as the query is concerned, we're done. However, as you'll recall, we still need a Clojure namespace to invoke YeSQL and have it parse our SQL file to generate the appropriate functions.

# Creating the albums model

In our example, YeSQL will generate a function called `get-recently-added`, which returns the 10 most recent-added albums added to hipstr.

To do this, we'll continue the same pattern we used for `user-model` and create an `album-model` namespace:

1. Alongside the `albums.sql` file, create a new Clojure file called `album_model.clj`.

2. Create the `hipstr.models.album-model` namespace, and load up the YeSQL library:

```
(ns hipstr.models.album-model
  (:require [yesql.core :refer [defqueries]]))
```

3. Again, we'll need to define our connection (don't worry, we're going to refactor it):

```
(def db-spec {:classname   "org.postgresql.Driver"
              :subprotocol "postgresql"
              :subname     "//localhost/postgres"
              :user        "hipstr"
              :password    "p455w0rd"})
```

4. Finally, we'll generate the annotated SQL functions using YeSQL's `defqueries`:

```
(defqueries "hipstr/models/albums.sql" {:connection db-spec})
```

At this point, our albums model is complete. Any other album-based data we want to retrieve from the database can be added as a YeSQL-generated function in the `albums.sql` file. However, there's one glaring, disgusting thing about this namespace that made me shudder and, hopefully, made you shudder as well – and that's the duplicate defined `db-spec`.

# Refactoring the connection

Don't Repeat Yourself (DRY). It's not just a good thing to do, and it should be your mantra as often as it makes sense. If we were to grow our hipstr application into a multi-billion dollar product with millions of users and hundreds of features, the last thing we'd want to do is define our database connection in every model. Let's refactor it by abstracting `db-spec` into its own namespace called `connection`:

1. In the same `hipstr/models` directory as the rest of our database-connectivity models and stuff, create another file called `connection.clj` and add the following:

```
(ns hipstr.models.connection)
```

2.  Move `db-spec` from the `hipstr.models.album-model` namespace into the `hisptr.models.connection` namespace:

```
(def db-spec {:classname   "org.postgresql.Driver"
              :subprotocol "postgresql"
              :subname     "//localhost/postgres"
              :user        "hipstr"
              :password    "p455w0rd"})
```

3.  Back in the `hipstr.models.album-model` namespace, add a reference to our new `hipstr.models.connection` namespace, and refer to `db-spec`:

```
(:require [yesql.core :refer [defqueries]]
          [hipstr.models.connection :refer [db-spec]]))
```

4.  Remove the `db-spec def` and repeat step 3 in the `hipstr.models.user-model` namespace.

So far, we've created the Migratus migration scripts to create our `artists` and `albums` tables and seed each with example data. We've also created a model layer using YeSQL that fetches data from those tables. We then refactored the common component, `db-spec`, out of the `user-model` and `album-model` and into its own namespace. Next up, we'll create a new Compojure route for serving the `recently-added` page.

# Creating the recently added route

Before we can view a page, we have to be able to serve it. We'll be creating a couple of album-related pages in hipstr. So let's create a new `hipstr.routes.albums` namespace, and also create a route to serve up a page for the `/albums/recently-added` URL:

1.  Create a new `hipstr.routes.albums` namespace in the `hipstr/routes` directory. As with our other route namespaces, we'll be making use of Compojure for creating the route, as well as `album-model` to retrieve the recently added albums from the database:

```
(ns hipstr.routes.albums
  (:require [compojure.core :refer :all]
            [hipstr.layout :as layout]
            [hipstr.models.album-model :as album]))
```

2. Next, we'll define a new `album-routes` defroute that will encapsulate all our albums-related routes for hipstr:

```
(defroutes album-routes
  (GET "/albums/recently-added" [] (album/get-recently-
  added)))
```

3. Finally, we have to add the new `album-routes` to the hipstr `app-handler`:

   1. Open the `hipstr/handler.clj` file and add a reference to the `hipstr.routes.albums` namespace we just created:

   ```
   (:require [compojure.core :refer [defroutes]]
             [hipstr.routes.albums :refer [album-routes]]
   ...)
   ```

   2. Add `album-routes` to the list of routes in `app-handler`:

   ```
   (def app (app-handler
     ;; add your application routes here
     [home-routes album-routes base-routes test-routes]
     ...))
   ```

At this point, we have enough plumbing to render the new route. Open your browser and navigate to `http://localhost:3000/albums/recently-added`, You should see the following as a result (or else, something similar, depending on how your browser renders straight JSON):

Hooray! Fortune is smiling upon us! Our new route is responding to requests, and is also making use of the `album-model` we created, which in turn uses YeSQL to fetch the 10 most recently added albums from the albums table (ordered by `create_date desc`). All the plumbing is there. The only thing we have left to do is represent this data in something a bit more palatable than straight up JSON.

# Rendering the results

We'll be using Selmer to render the *Recently Added* albums. We'll then display the rendered results instead of the crazy raw JSON.

Selmer templates, to refresh your memory, are stored in the `resources/templates` directory. As you may have guessed by now, I appreciate a nicely organized tree structure. So instead of throwing the `recently-added` template in with the rest of our templates, we'll create a new `albums` directory and house our album-related templates there:

1. Create a new directory, `albums`, in `resources/templates`.

2. Create a new Selmer template for our recently added albums, `resource/templates/albums/recently-added.html`, with the following content:

```
{% extends "templates/base.html" %}        <!-- 1 -->
{% block content %}                         <!-- 2 -->
<h1>Recently Added</h1>
<ol class="albums">
    {% for a in albums %}                   <!-- 3 -->
    <li>
        <div class="artist"><a href="/albums/{{a.artist}}">{{a.artist}}</a></div>
        <div class="album-name">{{a.album_name}}</div>
        <div class="release-date">{{a.release_date}}</div>
    </li>
    {% endfor %}
</ol>
{% endblock %}
```

The Selmer template we created is pretty basic. We're simply extending our `base.html` template (1), and providing content for the content block (2). For the actual content, we're using the Selmer `for` iterator (3) to render a list-item for each of the recently added albums, and then rendering the values of the various fields in each album.

 Consult *Chapter 4, URL Routing and Template Rendering*, if you need a little refresher on the basics of Selmer templates.

If you refresh the /albums/recently-added route in your browser, you'll find that it's... still JSON. That's because we're not yet rendering the previous template. Let's do that now:

1. Back in the hipstr.routes.albums namespace, create the following function (which invokes the Selmer rendering engine on our new template):

```
(defn recently-added-page
  "Renders out the recently-added page."
  []
  (layout/render "albums/recently-added.html"
    {:albums (album/get-recently-added)}))
```

2. Adjust our /albums/recently-added route to use the recently-added-page function, instead of the (album/get-recently-added) form:

```
(GET "/albums/recently-added" [] (recently-added-page))
```

Now refresh the /albums/recently-added route in your browser. You'll see the following gorgeous bit of HTML design genius:

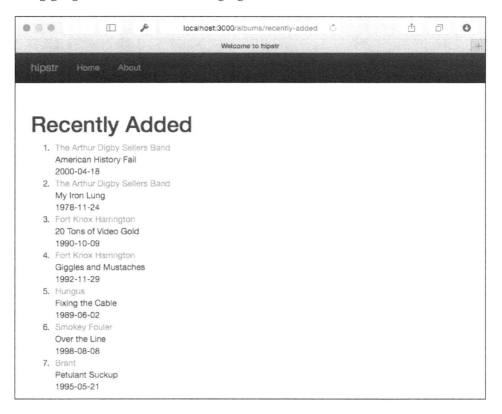

# An exercise!

So far, this chapter has been me giving you step-by-step lists of things to do. So if you're getting bored, I don't blame you. As such, I'm going to assign you some homework. You may have noticed that our recently added albums have a hyperlink for the band name.

Your task, if you choose to accept it (you should, it's super rad), is to create a second page. This page will be an artist's discography page. It will show all the albums by the artist that the user clicked. To accomplish this task you must perform the following steps:

1. Create the route to serve the artist page.
2. Create the YeSQL script to select all the albums for a given artist by name.
3. Create the template to render the list of albums for a given artist.

For example, clicking the Fort Knox Harrington link should produce the following:

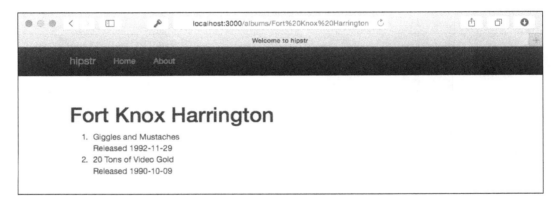

 In order to complete this task, you must use Compojure's parameter destructuring – See *Chapter 4, URL Routing and Template Rendering*, specifically the section on – surprise! – *Parameter destructuring*.

Try and give this a go. If you get stuck, you may consult the source code for this chapter. However, everything we've covered in this book up to this point is sufficient for you to create this page. Give it a whirl!

# Summary

In this chapter, we continued using Migratus to create additional tables in our database, as well as seed those tables with example data. We also used YeSQL to pull data from the database. We then created a couple of Selmer templates (assuming that you finished your homework) to display the albums and artists. In the next chapter, we will create forms for adding artists and albums to the database, and also learn how to do it safely inside a transaction.

# 9
# Database Transactions

In the previous chapter, we continued our use of Migratus migration scripts to create the bleeding-edge hipstr catalog (the *artists* and *albums* tables). We also created some YeSQL functions that pulled the catalog data from the database, and rendered it to the screen with such beauty and poise that I wouldn't be surprised if we got a job tomorrow at a rather massive Silicon Valley company.

This chapter will continue along the same vein as the previous: more coding, fewer fun ogre boring things. In this chapter we will cover the following topics:

- Learning what a database transaction is, and why it's important
- How database transactions look in Clojure, and how they can be applied when using YeSQL
- Creating a form that accepts an artist name, album name, and release date, and how to store it in the database using a transaction

This chapter will use everything we've learned so far in the book, including validations using **Validateur**, routes using Compojure, and YeSQL for more goodness. But before we get started we should probably review what a database transaction is.

# Introduction to Database Transactions

Sometimes I like to see what the internet says about a particular topic, and then spend a few hours trying to make sense of it. Let's take a look at what Wikipedia says about database transactions:

> *"A transaction comprises a unit of work performed within a database management system (or similar system) against a database, and treated in a coherent and reliable way independent of other transactions... A database transaction, by definition, must be atomic, consistent, isolated and durable."*

> -http://en.wikipedia.org/wiki/Database_transaction

I'm not going to lie. I hate computer jargon. It's always a mouthful, and, more often than not, leaves me confused. The essence of the preceding quote can be put simply thus: A database transaction is a bunch of work which is either completed in its entirety or isn't performed at all, and, in the process, doesn't screw anything else up. It's all-or-nothing, while respecting its neighbors. That's the easy version. Read on for the more in-depth version.

# The ACID properties

The official definition of the set of properties governing database transactions is mentioned as **Atomic**, **Consistent**, **Isolated**, and **Durable** (known as **ACID**). These are the four tenants of a database transaction. Broken down, they mean the following:

- **Atomic**: All work that must be performed by the database inside a transaction – that is, reading data, deleting data, updating data, and/or inserting data – is treated as a single unit of work. It's literally all-or-nothing. If anything fails, then it all fails, and you revert back to the way the universe was before you'd gone and mucked it all up.

- **Consistent** – This is basically *The Principle of Least Astonishment*; that is, there are no surprises, and everything is as you expect it to be. Foreign keys and other constraints are respected, the state of the data prior to the transaction is used within the transaction, etc. In short a transaction should never, ever leave you with the thought, *Huh, how did that happen?!*

- **Isolated**: It determines just how much of your transaction you want other users of the database to see, and when. For example, perhaps you still want to give others read access to the data while you manipulate it, or maybe you want exclusive access to it until you're done. There's a trade-off for each. Basically, isolation is to database transactions what window curtains are to you when walking around your apartment naked.

- **Durable**: This means that when the transaction is complete and *committed*, the state of that data is there to stay. It's permanent. Even if you've screwed it up. So don't screw it up.

Ultimately, ACID can be boiled down to a very simple concept: Guaranteed to work, or nothing at all.

# Importance of database transactions

If you were writing a tiny app for yourself that only you were using, it's arguable that database transactions are a needless overhead. However, in an environment such as the Web, where multiple users are likely accessing the same data at the same time while data manipulations are occurring, database transactions are a good thing. You want your data to be consistent and valid. For without database transactions, a system under heavy use would lose all data integrity before you finished reading this sentence. I may or may not know this first hand.

# Implementing a transaction

Implementing a transaction in Clojure, while using YeSQL, is about as trivial a thing as picking lint out of your belly button. Pretend, for instance, that we had the following database table called `fun_ogres` (hint: you can follow along using your own `psql` instance if you so desire):

We could create a YeSQL function such as the following:

```
-- name: insert-ogre<!
-- Adds a new fun-ogre to our database.
INSERT INTO fun_ogres (ogre_id, name, specialty)
VALUES (:ogre_id, :name, :specialty)
```

Of course, as you've seen, you could then call the preceding YeSQL-generated function from a Clojure namespace by simply doing the following:

```
(require '[yesql.core :refer [defquery]])
(def some-db-spec {...})
(defqueries "some/path/fun_ogres.sql" {:connection some-db-spec})
(insert-ogre<! {:ogre_id 1 :name "Debby Downer"
  :specialty "Never laughs at jokes. Ever."})
```

We've seen this pattern about a half-dozen times now, as we've done it for all of our data so far. It works, and it works fine. However, pretend we were importing a few fun_ogres, such as the following:

```
(def ogres-to-import
  [{:ogre_id 1 :name "Debby Downer"
    :specialty "Never laughs at jokes. Ever."}
   {:ogre_id 2 :name "Droopy David"
    :specialty "He loves to sulk in public."}
   {:ogre_id 3 :name "Crabby Colin"
    :specialty "Constantly complaining about everything."}])
(doseq [ogre ogres-to-import]
  (insert-ogre<! ogre))
```

Let's say, for whatever reason (perhaps a network hiccup or a zombie attack), that our insert fails between Droopy David and Crabby Colin. At this point, our application fails. And the next time we try and import the ogres, our doseq is going to fail immediately on the first insert due to a primary key violation. This is because we successfully inserted the first two fun ogres, and then they lived up to their name, and we failed to insert the third one. This is because we weren't running our inserts in a transaction, and thus, atomicity was not guaranteed.

# Transactions in Clojure

Creating a transaction in Clojure is simple; we just use the native clojure.java.jdbc/with-db-transaction macro. We pass it our connection settings, and then we get a handle to a transaction – similar to the following:

```
(require '[clojure.java.jdbc :as jdbc])
(jdbc/with-db-transaction [tx some-db-spec]
  ; perform a bunch of stuff inside a transaction
  ) ; commit
```

If all the code inside the with-db-transaction form completes successfully, the transaction will be automatically committed for us. If anything fails, it will rollback and an exception will be raised. This is about as straightforward as you can get. However, how do we tell YeSQL to make use of the transaction?

# Transactions in YeSQL

If you recall, in Chapter 7, *Getting Started with the Database*, we very briefly discussed that there were 2 ways we could define a connection with YeSQL:

- Define the connection options as part of the call to the defqueries function, and/or

- Pass the connection when making the actual call to the YeSQL function

So far in this book, we've been utilizing the first option. However, if we want to use a transaction within YeSQL, we have to make use of the second option. To facilitate this, we have to use with-db-transaction to create a transaction context, and then pass that transaction context into the call to insert-ogre<!. Our fancy import, then, would be slightly modified to the following:

```
(require '[yesql.core :refer [defquery]]
         '[clojure.java.jdbc :as jdbc])                    ;#1
(def ogres-to-import
  [{:ogre_id 1 :name "Debby Downer"
    :specialty "Never laughs at jokes. Ever."}
   {:ogre_id 2 :name "Droopy David"
    :specialty "He loves to sulk in public."}
   {:ogre_id 3 :name "Crabby Colin"
    :specialty "Constantly complaining about everything."}])
(jdbc/with-db-transaction [tx some-db-spec]                ;#2
  (doseq [ogre ogres-to-import]
    (insert-ogre<! ogre {:connection tx})))                ;#3
```

The only changes we made were the following:

- #1: This imports the clojure.java.jdbc namespace so we can use it

- #2: This wraps our doseq within the context of a transaction

- #3: This passes the transaction handle tx into the YeSQL-generated function insert-ogre<! as the final argument

Now, if anything inside the transaction context fails for any reason, the transaction will be rolled back and none of the fun ogres will be inserted.

That is literally (almost) all there is to using transactions in Clojure and YeSQL. The rest of this chapter will mostly be code, extending our hipstr application such that we can submit a new artist and album, as well as create those entries on demand if necessary, all within the context of a transaction.

You can read more about JDBC transactions in Clojure by checking out the rather useful documentation at: http://clojure.github.io/java.jdbc/

# Extending the application requirements in brief

Our pointy-haired marketing wizard (me) has decided that our hipstr application requires the ability to add a new artist and album (with a release date). The form should be validated, ensuring that all of the data is appropriate, before sending it off to the database. If, for whatever reason, the inserts into the database fail, then nothing should be changed. Also, if there are any validation errors with the form, we want to show an appropriate message to the user. Finally, I want to be able to use this form anywhere in the site with minimal modifications and maximum code reuse. (*Say whaaaaaaat?!*)

# Creating the add artist/album form

Let's brainstorm what this magical and revolutionary piece of functionality should look like. Based on what currently exists, the following idea should suffice:

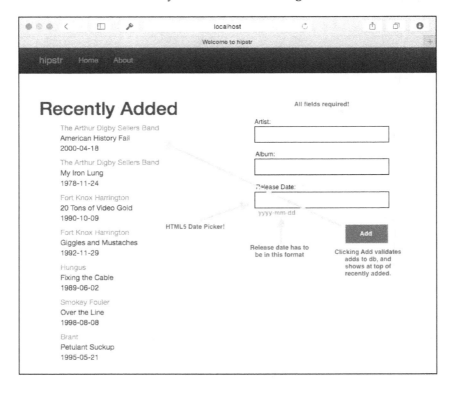

This seems pretty doable, and it satisfies all of our requirements. First things first though: Let's create the HTML for the form.

# Creating the form

We'll assume that the expected data structure against which this form will be bound is the following:

```
{:form {:error "" ; For reporting any error that's not a
                  ; validation error
       :validation-errors { :artist_name #{}
                            :album_name #{}
                            :release_date #{}
       :new {:artist_name "" :album_name "" :release_date ""}
```

For now, we just want to extend our existing `recently-added.html` template. That's the quickest entry point. Open the `resources/templates/albums/recently-added.html` template, and add the additional, bolded HTML shown as follows:

```
{% extends "templates/base.html" %}
{% block content %}
<h1>Recently Added</h1>
<div class="row">
<div class="col-sm-6 col-md-4">
  <ol class="albums">
    {% for a in albums %}
    <li>
      <div class="artist"><a href="/albums/{{a.artist}}">{{a.artist}}</a></div>
      <div class="album-name">{{a.album_name}}</div>
      <div class="release-date">{{a.release_date}}</div>
    </li>
    {% endfor %}

  </ol>
</div>
<div class="col-sm-6 col-md-4">
  {% if form.error %}                              <!-- #1 -->
  <p class="bg-danger">{{form.error}}</p>
  {% endif %}
  <form role="form" method="post" class="add-album">
    <div class="form-group">
      <label for="artist_name">Artist</label>
      <ul class="errors">
```

```
            {% for e in form.validation-errors.artist_name %}
            <li>{{e}}</li>
            {% endfor %}
        </ul>
        <input type="input" name="artist_name" class="form-control"
id="artist_name" value="{{ form.new.artist_name }}">
        </div>
        <div class="form-group">
          <label for="album_name">Album</label>
          <ul class="errors">
            {% for e in form.validation-errors.album_name %}
            <li>{{e}}</li>
            {% endfor %}
          </ul>
          <input type="input" name="album_name" class="form-control"
id="album_name" value="{{ form.new.album_name }}">
        </div>
        <div class="form-group">
          <label for="release_date">Release Date</label>
          <ul class="errors">
            {% for e in form.validation-errors.release_date %}
            <li>{{e}}</li>
            {% endfor %}
          </ul>
          <input type="date" name="release_date" class="form-control"
id="release_date" value="{{ form.new.release_date }}">
          <p class="help-block">yyyy-mm-dd</p>
        </div>
        <div class="form-group submit">
          <button type="submit" class="btn btn-primary">Add</button>
        </div>
      </form>
    </div>
{% endblock %}
```

Everything in here looks pretty familiar. We simply extended our Selmer template to include the form. The only interesting part is at #1, where we make use of the `{% if %}` tag. Anything inside the `{% if [condition] %}{% endif %}` block is only rendered if the `[condition]` evaluates to something truthy (that is, not `nil`, or an actual `true` Boolean value). Other than that, this seems very similar to our User Sign Up form; we have a list of potential errors for each field, and we are binding the value for each of our inputs to the values in the `form.new` context map.

Save the file and navigate to `http://localhost:3000/albums/recently-added`, then pick your jaw up off the floor after you feast your eyes on the wondrous marvel that is the following:

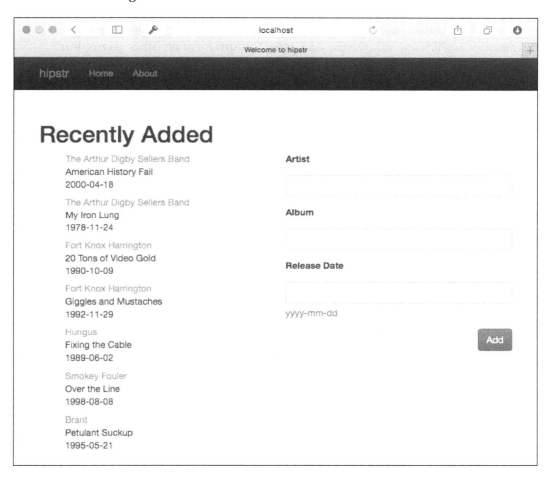

 You can get the right-alignment of the Add button by including the following CSS in the `resources/public/css/screen.css` file:

`.submit{ text-align: right; }`

This looks strikingly like the mock-up we came up with. Meaning: Success! However, there's a catch.

# Abstracting the form

One of the requirements that got snuck in was the following: *Finally, I want to be able to use this form anywhere in the site with minimal modifications and maximum code reuse.*

Hmmm. If that's the case, then the HTML code we created isn't up to snuff. It's possible we'll want to have the add artist/album form on other pages, but we're unlikely to want to copy and paste the form code every time. That's gross. Thankfully, Selmer provides a couple of tags that we can use in conjunction with each other to abstract the form and load it wherever we want. Those tags are **with** and **include**. They are explained as follows:

- **with**: The with block allows us to define scope. Any keys we define in the `with` tag will be available to anything inside the `with` block.
- **include**: The `include` block allows us to dynamically compile and inject external templates.

With the preceding tags in mind, we can actually abstract our form into its own separate Selmer template. Let's do that now:

1. Create a new Selmer template alongside our `recently-added` HTML template, `resources/templates/albums/add-album.html`

2. Move the DOM inside the second `<div class="col-sm-6 col-md-4">` code, from the `recently-added.html` template, into the `add-album.html` template so that `add-album.html` looks like the following:

```
{% if form.error %}
<p class="bg-danger error">{{form.error}}</p>
{% endif %}
<form role="form" method="post" class="add-album">
  <!-- snipped for brevity -->
</form>
```

3. Inside the now empty `div` tag, use the `include` tag to load our `add-album.html`, and wrap it inside a `with` block:

```
<div class="col-sm-6 col-md-4">
  {% with form=form %}
  {% include "templates/albums/add-album.html" %}
  {% endwith %}
</div>
```

The `include` function tells Selmer, "*Hey*, compile the `templates/albums/add-album.html` template and load its contents here." The `with` block passes the context to the included template; in this case, the expected `:form` data structure we outlined at the start of creating the form.

When we refresh the page we should see absolutely no visual difference.

# Creating the add artist/album endpoint

Now that we have the form in place, we need to set up the route against which the form will POST. Since we don't currently have a target attribute on the form, the form will simply POST to whatever the current URL is. For the purpose of this exercise, we'll allow that. As such, we'll need to define a Compojure route for `/albums/recently-added` that will accept the form input, validate it, add the data to the database, and then re-render the page. Of course, we'll break all this up across multiple namespaces, because we're good developers like that, and because we fear the wrath of our cubicle mates.

## Creating the Compojure route

Let's create the Compojure route. In the `hipstr.routes.albums` namespace, add the following to our `album-routes`:

```
(POST "/albums/recently-added" [& album-form]
  (recently-added-submit album-form))
```

As the route alludes, we next want to create a function for handling the actual POSTed data – hence the need to create a `recently-added-submit` function.

## Creating the route helper function

The `recently-added-submit` function will validate the information submitted by the user, and then render the `recently-added.html` template. It will also take into account the form's expected data structure, as well as the data required for generating the recently-added-albums list:

```
(defn recently-added-submit
  "Handles the add-album form on the recently-added page.
   In the case of validation errors or other unexpected errors,
   the :new key in the context will be set to the album
   information submitted by the user."
  [album]
  (let [errors (v/validate-new-album album)            ;#1
        form-ctx (if (not-empty errors)
                   {:validation-errors errors :new album}  ;#2
                   (try
                     (album/add-album! album)           ;#3
                     {:new {} :success true}
                     (catch Exception e
                       (timbre/error e)
```

```
                          {:new album
                           :error "Oh snap! We lost the album. Try it
                           again?"}))))                        ;#3.1
          ctx (merge {:form form-ctx}
                     {:albums (album/get-recently-added)})]     ;#4
      (layout/render "albums/recently-added.html" ctx))        ;#5
```

We'll also need to adjust the required libraries in our namespace definition. Add the following to the :require in our namespace definition:

```
(:require ...
          [hipstr.validators.album-validator :as v]
          [taoensso.timbre :as timbre])
```

In the preceding code we've taken the strategy of constructing the context that we'll pass to the template being rendered. The very last thing we do is actually render the template. The basic algorithm for the preceding code is as follows:

1.  Validate the input for errors.
2.  If the input fails to validate, set those validation errors on the context, along with the user submitted data (this way they don't have to re-type their data, and they can see what was actually invalid).
3.  Otherwise, attempt to add the album, and provide a success flag on the context when successful.
    ○   If adding the album fails for any reason, include the submitted data on the context, as well as a simple error message
4.  Add the recently added albums to the context.
5.  Render the template.

There are a thousand ways we could have done this. Feel free to try your own ideas! But for now, this algorithm and implementation seem pretty sound. There's one thing we may want to consider however, and that's the fact that our hipstr.routes.albums namespace now has 2 calls to render the same template in 2 different locations. Kind of yucky. Let's abstract that out to its own function, render-recently-added-html, which accepts the context:

```
(defn render-recently-added-html
  "Simply renders the recently added page with the given context."
  [ctx]
  (layout/render "albums/recently-added.html" ctx))

(defn recently-added-page
```

```
    "Renders out the recently-added page."
    []
    (render-recently-added-html {:albums (album/get-recently-added)}))

(defn recently-added-submit
  ;… snipped for brevity…
    (render-recently-added-html ctx)))
```

We could probably employ further patterns to reduce things like the call to `album/get-recently-added`, but for now this seems pretty good. What we absolutely must do in order for this to work, however, is the following:

1. Write the `validate-new-album` validator (`v/validate-new-album`).

2. Include the album validator as a requirement.

3. Write the function to add the actual album to the database (`album/add-album!`).

# Validating the add artist/album form

In Chapter 5, *Handling Form Input*, we were introduced to Validateur, a simple library that allows us to validate user input, as well as provide specific error messages for input that is invalid. In this section, we'll use Validateur again to write some validations for new albums.

Create the new namespace, `hipstr.validators.album`, and add to that file the following code:

```
(ns hipstr.validators.album
  (:require [validateur.validation :refer :all]
            [noir.validation :as v]
            [clj-time.core :as t]
            [clj-time.format :as f]))
```

 The `clj-time` library provides us a sane way of working with dates. At a high level, it wraps the Joda-Time library. The `clj-time` library is already on our classpath as it's a dependency of `im.chit/cronj` included with Luminus projects. You can read more about clj-time at https://github.com/clj-time/clj-time and Joda-Time at http://www.joda.org/joda-time/.

The artist and album fields on our form are mandatory, but will allow any character. However, our database schema does have a 255 character limit on both the artist and the album columns.

If you can't remember the schema definition for a table in PostgreSQL, you can run \d [table-name] inside psql and it will show you a (reasonably) formatted description of the tables:

With that in mind, let's write the artist validation first, ensuring that the artist name is an acceptable specific length:

```
(def artist-name-validations
  "Returns a validation set, ensuring an artist name is valid."
  (validation-set
    (length-of :artist_name :within (range 1 256)
               :message-fn (fn [type m attributes & args]
                             (if (= type :blank)
                               "Artist name is required."
                               "Artist name must be less than 255
                                characters long.")))))
```

The preceding code should look familiar as it's very similar to the username validation in the hipstr.validators.user-validator namespace. The artist-name-validations def returns a validation set that implicitly ensures that something other than blank values makes up the artist name (the default behavior for length-of), and that the name length is a maximum of 255 characters long. We'll add the same for the album name:

```
(def album-name-validations
  (validation-set
    (length-of :album_name :within (range 1 256)
               :message-fn (fn [type m attributes & args]
                             (if (= type :blank)
                               "Album name is required."
                               "Album name must be less than 255
                                characters long.")))))
```

The release date validator is slightly more complex. Not only must the release date meet a specific format (year-month-day), it must also be a real date (there's no 13th month or 32nd day in July, for example). Ensuring the format of the data is easy, since we can use the `format-of` validator and a simple regular expression:

```
(def release-date-format-message
  "The release date's format is incorrect. Must be yyyy-mm-dd.")

(def release-date-invalid-message
  "The release date is not a valid date.")

(def release-date-format-validator
  "Returns a validator function which ensures the format of the
   date-string is correct."
  (format-of :release_date
             :format #"^\d{4}-\d{2}-\d{2}$"
             :blank-message release-date-format-message
             :message release-date-format-message))
```

Again, this should look somewhat familiar, as we also used the `format-of` validator to ensure that a submitted username is of the proper format.

Ensuring a date is valid, however, requires a bit more thought. Firstly, there's no point in validating the release date if the format of the date string is invalid. Secondly, we need to ensure the date is *parseable* and valid. To do this, we'll use some of Clojure's date/time libraries, as well as Validateurs's `validate-when` predicate.

The `validate-when` function returns a function that will run a validator if, and only if, a provided predicate returns true. You can think of `validate-when` as Validateur's "if predicate true, then do such and such". In our case, we only want to validate the release date when it's in the correct format. As such, we can leverage our `release-date-format-validator` to be the predicate for `validate-when`:

```
(def release-date-formatter
  (f/formatter "yyyy-mm-dd"))

(defn parse-date
  "Returns a date/time object if the provided date-string is
   valid; otherwise nil."
  [date]
  (try
    (f/parse release-date-formatter date)
    (catch Exception e)))
```

```
(def release-date-validator
  "Returns a validator function which ensures the provided
   date-string is a valid date."
  (validate-when #(valid? (validation-set
                    release-date-format-validator) %)
                 (validate-with-predicate :release_date
                  #(v/not-nil? (parse-date (:release_date %)))
                  :message release-date-invalid-message)))
```

In the preceding code, the `validateur.validation.valid?` is our test condition, and, only when its result is true, will our `validate-with-predicate` actually be executed. The `validate-with-predicate` validator ensures that `parse-date` returns something other than nil, which will only occur if `parse-date` fails to parse the date string (a result of the date string either not being in the expected format or not being a real date).

Finally, we can wrap these up into a simple, easy-to-use validation set:

```
(def release-date-validations
  "Returns a validator which, when the format of the date-string
   is correct, ensures the date itself is valid."
  (validation-set release-date-format-validator
                  release-date-validator))
```

The last thing to do, now that we have all this wonderfully modular code, is to create the `validate-new-album` validation set which will be used from the `hipstr.routes.album/recently-added-submit` function:

```
(def validate-new-album
  "Returns a validator that knows how to validate all the fields
   for a new album."
  (compose-sets artist-name-validations album-name-validations
                release-date-validations))
```

Phew! Data validation…Always the most tedious thing. Users should just know, shouldn't they? Either way, we're done! The last thing we need to do is expand our `hipstr.models.album-model` to include the `add-album!` function.

# Expanding the album model

Currently, our `hipstr.models.album-model` namespace defers everything to the YeSQL-generated queries from the `hipstr/models/albums.sql` file. This is fine, as we will leverage it to add a couple new functions. However, because our constraints are such that `album.artist_id` is a foreign key to `artist.artist_id`, we must have the means of inserting a new artist. As such, we'll create a new SQL file, `hipstr/models/artists.sql`.

The first function we'll define in the `artists.sql` file is the `insert-artist<!` function:

```
-- name: insert-artist<!
-- Inserts a new artist into the database.
-- Expects :name.
INSERT INTO artists(name)
VALUES (:artist_name);
```

The artist name is the only value we need to provide because everything else in the `artists` table is generated for us by PostgresSQL. The `create_at` and `update_at` field values are handled by our trigger, and `artist_id` is handled by Postgres because we defined it to be SERIAL (that is, an auto-incrementing integer). Great! However, you may be wondering (and possibly groaning), "Do we need to create a `hipstr.models1.artist-model` now?" To which I reply, "No."

There is nothing prohibiting us from making multiple calls to YeSQL's `defqueries` function and passing it a different SQL file each time. In this spirit, we can generate multiple functions across multiple tables in the current namespace. As such, the only thing we need to do in order to make use of our shiny new `insert-artist<!` function is tell YeSQL to make use of it. Add the following to the `hipstr.models.album-model` namespace:

```
(defqueries "hipstr/models/albums.sql" {:connection db-spec})

(defqueries "hipstr/models/artists.sql" {:connection db-spec})
```

YeSQL will generate functions for both SQL files and load them into the current namespace, and by default run any SQL queries using the same database specification (`db-spec`). With that in mind, let's add the `insert-album<!` function to the `hipstr/models/albums.sql` file as well. Add the following:

```
-- name: insert-album<!
-- Adds the album for the given artist to the database
-- EXPECTS :artist_id, :album_name, and :release_date
INSERT INTO albums (artist_id, name, release_date)
VALUES (:artist_id, :album_name, date(:release_date));
```

Again, this is a pretty straightforward insert statement. Life is easy in these parts of the woods. Now that we have those queries available for generation, let's make use of them.

Back in the `hipstr.models.album` namespace, add a new (and dare I say, first!) function, `add-album!`, which will accept the same information posted from our Add artist/album form; that is `{:artist_name :album_name :release_date}`. The first iteration of this function will blindly add the artist and album to our database:

```
(defn add-album!
  "Adds a new album to the database."
  [album]
  (let [artist-info (insert-artist<!
          {:artist_name (:artist_name album)})]
    (insert-album<! (assoc album :artist_id
                      (:artist_id artist-info)))))
```

The preceding code is pretty simple. Add the artist, associate the new `artist_id` with the album, and then insert the album. This works like gravy on potatoes until you try to add a second album by the same artist (our UNIQUE INDEX constraint on the `artists.name` column will make sure of that). The same thing will happen if we try to add an album of the same name by the same artist, as we have a UNIQUE INDEX spanning the `albums.artist_id` and `albums.name` columns.

The requirements don't state to throw an exception if the artist or album already exists. And frankly, I don't see the point. Let's not be wasteful and just make use of the already existing artist/album, if that's the case. This implies, of course, that we have a way of getting the artist or album, by name, from the database. No sweat! Let's add a `get-artists-by-name` to our `artists.sql` file:

```
-- name: get-artists-by-name
-- Retrieves an artist from the database by name.
-- Expects :artist_name
SELECT *
FROM artists
WHERE name=:artist_name;
```

Similarly, let's add the `get-albums-by-name` query to our `albums.sql` file:

```
-- name: get-albums-by-name
-- Fetches the specific album from the database for a particular
-- artist.
-- Expects :artist_id and :album_name.
SELECT *
FROM albums
WHERE
  artist_id = :artist_id and
  name = :album_name;
```

Again, not a whole lot of surprises here. We include an `artist_id` in the WHERE clause so we can limit the scope of the albums returned.

Lets get back to our `hisptr.models.album-model/add-album!` function. Now that we have a couple more queries, let's make use of them to avoid the pitfalls of duplicate artist/albums. Adjust the function so that it resembles the following:

```
(defn add-album!
  "Adds a new album to the database."
  [album]
  (let [artist-info {:artist_name (:artist_name album)}
        ; fetch or insert the artist record
        artist (or (first (get-artists-by-name artist-info))   ;#1
                   (insert-artist<! artist-info))
        album-info (assoc album :artist_id (:artist_id artist))]
    (or (first (get-album-by-name album-info))                 ;#2
        (insert-album<! album-info))))
```

In the preceding code, we're now checking that an artist or album exists and, if not, we add them. The only thing that might stump us is the call to `first` at #1 and #2. Despite the logic of the query and the schema guaranteeing only 1 or zero returned rows, we'll still need to make a call to `first` because query results are always returned as a sequence. Remember, YeSQL isn't *intelligent*; it's not examining the schema or query and making necessary adjustments, it's merely generating Clojure functions which map back to the SQL for us.

We now have a model function which makes use of an already existing artist/album and inserts only when required. However, there's one glaring hole: it's not in a transaction. The function could, in theory, successfully insert an artist, and then fail when inserting the album, which isn't what we would expect from such a form. Let's ensure that doesn't happen.

# Wrapping the whole thing in a transaction

At the start of this chapter, we learned that wrapping YeSQL functions inside a transaction is trivial. Every YeSQL-generated function takes, as its second (optional) argument, an alternate connection, which can be a handle to an existing transaction. We can pass a transaction context, generated by `clojure.java.jdbc/with-db-transaction`, as the second parameter.

First, add a reference to the `clojure.java.jdbc` library at the top in our `:require`:

```
(:require [clojure.java.jdbc :as jdbc]
  ...)
```

Secondly, wrap the body of `add-album!` inside the call to `with-db-transaction`:

```
(defn add-album!
  "Adds a new album to the database."
  [album]
  (jdbc/with-db-transaction [tx db-spec]                     ;#1
    (let [artist-info {:artist_name (:artist_name album)}
          txn {:connection tx}                               ;#2
          ; fetch or insert the artist record
          artist (or (first (get-artist-by-name artist-info txn))
                     (insert-artist<! artist-info txn))
          album-info (assoc album :artist_id (:artist_id artist))]
      (or (first (get-albums-by-name album-info txn))
          (insert-album<! album-info txn)))))
```

At #1, in the preceding code, we get a new transaction handle, `tx`, from the `jdbc` library; and then, at #2, we create a connection map to use the `tx` transaction handle. All of our subsequent calls to YeSQL then use the `txn` connection map. And that's it! The `add-album!` is now fully wrapped inside a transaction. Go ahead and fail, world! But there is one, single, tiny improvement we can make.

## Using a transaction outside of this scope

A downfall to our preceding transaction code is that it will never allow any transaction other than its own. We are good programming citizens, cognizant of the needs of others. And it's quite possible there will be cases wherein `add-album!` will be part of a larger transaction. We can support this by making use of arity overloading. Modify the `add-album!` function such that it accepts multiple arities: one that accepts only an album, and another that accepts an album and a connection:

```
(defn add-album!
  "Adds a new album to the database."
  ([album]
   (jdbc/with-db-transaction [tx db-spec]
     (add-album! album tx)))
  ([album tx]                                                ; #1
   (let [artist-info {:artist_name (:artist_name album)}
         txn {:connection tx}
         ; fetch or insert the artist record
         artist (or (first (get-artist-by-name artist-info txn))
                    (insert-artist<! artist-info txn))
         album-info (assoc album :artist_id (:artist_id artist))]
     (or (first (get-album-by-name album-info txn))
         (insert-album<! album-info txn)))))
```

The preceding code extracts the meat of the add-album! function into its own arity (#1), which accepts the album to be inserted and a second, alternate connection. The downside of this pattern is that the connection parameter (tx) doesn't have to be a transaction. Thus, clients of this code now have the ability to add an album in a non-transaction state. But that's okay, sometimes you need to give somebody the power to shoot themselves in the foot in order for them to learn.

# Summary

This was a fairly comprehensive chapter. We learned what a database transaction is, the core tenants of a database transaction (ACID), and how you can use transactions in Clojure and YeSQL. We utilized everything we've covered in the book so far. It was intense. We will continue the comprehensive example style into the next chapter, where we will (finally) authenticate and authorize users.

# 10
# Sessions and Cookies

In the last chapter, we conquered database transactions. We extended our hipstr application to use them, and it worked, and it was good. If you've been paying attention (and I'm sure you have because it's Chapter 10 and we're almost done), you'll have noticed that we've yet to actually authenticate our user, create a session, or write any cookies. Well, I've got news for you: In this chapter, we're going to do all three of those things! That is, we're going to cover the following topics in this chapter:

- Learn about sessions and how they're maintained in Luminus and Noir
- Build a form to authenticate our user
- Create a cookie that remembers the username for the next time a user wants to login

We'll start off with a bit of how these things are accomplished in Luminus (and the underlying `lib-noir` library), and then extend our hipstr application to embrace these missing components.

## Sessions

HTTP, the foundation of the web as we know it, is stateless. This means that every request is independent of any previous request. In the world of HTTP, each request has a matching response. We see independent requests everywhere in HTTP; requesting a static resource, a web page, or an AJAX request are all examples of the stateless protocol in action.

That being said, we still require the ability to track users across requests. Without some type of unique tracking of the person or system sending the request, we wouldn't be able to have authenticated-only pages, partition user data, or a zillion other things. Sessions allow us to track information about the sender between each request.

In our hipstr app, this is tied together by a cookie called, *ring-session*. You can view the cookie by navigating to the hipstr app on your machine (`http://localhost:3000`, by default). You can then open the development tools in your browser and, typically, view the resources for the page. Typically, there's a **Cookies** section in there, and you can view which cookies for the current site exist in your browser. In Safari, you'll see the following screenshot:

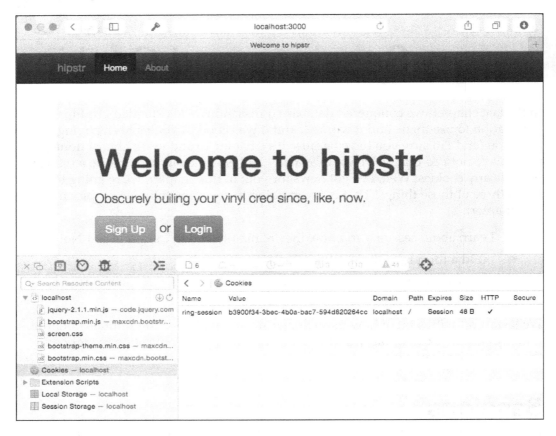

Likewise, in Chrome, you'll see something like the following screenshot:

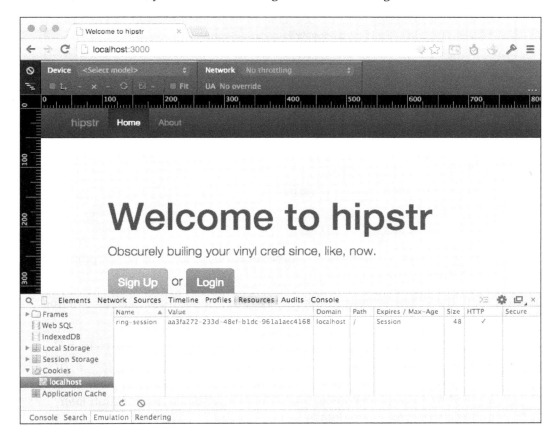

In Internet Explorer…well, honestly, I've not used it in almost a decade. But I think you can hit *Ctrl + F12* and do an Irish jig or something, and it'll tell you what you need to know.

The `ring-session` cookie is written out on the first request and lasts for the lifetime of the browser. The writing of the cookie is handled for us automatically – in fact, all of the session setup and management is handled for us automatically. In *Chapter 2, Ring and the Ring Server,* we talked about the Luminus-generated `hipstr.handler` namespace, in which there is a call to *app-handler* that is used to package up the hipstr application handler. On the surface, the `app-handler` seems like a fairly simple thing. Behind the scenes, however, it's tying together a lot of different middlewares (both `lib-noir` and Ring middlewares) and functionality, including session and cookie management.

For the curious: The `ring-defaults` library, way deep under
the hood, has quite the middleware. You can take a peak at it here:
`https://github.com/ring-clojure/ring-defaults/`
`blob/master/src/ring/middleware/defaults.clj`

# Setting up sessions

By default, Luminus generates our app to use an in-memory session store with
adequate defaults. The session default settings are specified in the `hipstr.handler/`
`session-defaults`:

```
;; timeout sessions after 30 minutes
(def session-defaults
  {:timeout (* 60 30)
     :timeout-response (redirect "/")})
```

The preceding code sets default session-timeout to 30 minutes, at which point the
user will be redirected to root (/).

In addition to the `:timeout` and `:timeout-response` options, we can also define
the following:

- `:cookie-name` [string]: This is the name for the session cookie (which
  defaults to *ring-session*)

- `:cookie-attrs` [map]: This is a map of standard cookie options to be
  applied to the session cookie. See *Setting the cookie as a map* section later
  in this chapter for more details

- `:store`: This allows us to define an alternate store to the default in-memory
  session store. Setting up an alternative to the in-memory session store is
  beyond the scope of this book.

Note: If you're curious about setting up an alternative to the in-memory
session store, I strongly recommend using Redis (an incredible, open
source data structure server - `http://www.redis.io`). You can
use Redis as a session store by using Carmine (which is an open
source Clojure client library for Redis - `https://github.com/`
`ptaoussanis/carmine`).

For the purpose of our example application, the in-memory session store will more
than suffice. But how do we use it?

# Interacting with the session

Fetching and retrieving information to and from the session in noir is easy. The noir.session namespace is our main interface, which mostly contains functions to store and retrieve data in the session, as well as some wrappers and cleanup functions. Initially, a noir session is just an empty map.

We can store data in the current session by entering the following:

```
(require '[noir.session :as session])
(session/put! :foo "baaaaaaaarrrrrr!")
>> {:foo "baaaaaaaarrrrrr"}
```

We can then retrieve a value from the session using get, as in the following:

```
(session/get :foo)
>> "baaaaaaaarrrrrr"
```

We can also use assoc-in! to associate a nested key/value pair, and any level that doesn't exist will be initialized as an empty map on our behalf:

```
(session/assoc-in! [:some :nested] "hey there, I need some air down here.")
>> {:foo "baaaaaaaarrrrrr" :some {:nested "hey there, I need some air down here."}}
```

Likewise, we can retrieve the nested structure by using get-in and passing it a vector of keys:

```
(session/get-in [:some :nested])
>> "hey there, I need some air down here."
```

We can also blow away all the data in our session by using clear! function:

```
(session/clear!)
>> {}
```

These are the basics of interacting with the session, and, for the purpose of hipstr, are all we require. However, there is much more functionality provided by the noir.session namespace. You can get a comprehensive list of noir.session functionality by viewing the source code at https://github.com/noir-clojure/lib-noir/blob/master/src/noir/session.clj. Don't be afraid, it's actually quite well documented and pretty straightforward.

# Restricted routes

Restricting access to a specific web page or some functionality is a cornerstone of today's web apps. Without restricting resources or functionality, the applications that power the Internet would be in complete anarchy. Anybody could post as anybody on Twitter; Facebook would suddenly have 1 single user representing 1/7th of the world's population; YouTube would become even more dominated by cats. Hence, restricting access is a good thing – even if you wish YouTube was dominated (even more so) by cats.

Restricting routes in a Luminus application is a two pronged approach. First, we must mark a route as restricted. Secondly, we must define what governs access to the restricted route.

# Restricting route access

There are two ways we can restrict route access in a Luminus app. The first is by using the `noir.util.route/restricted` macro on the route in question. For example, pretend we had the following route:

```
(GET "/just-for-you" [] (render-private-page))
```

That's something we've seen no fewer than a dozen times. In its current incarnation, anybody and everybody can view /just-for-you as it has no restrictions. It's wide open and public. It is the exact opposite of just-for-you. We can lock this down by applying the `restricted` macro, as seen here:

```
(require '[noir.util.route :refer [restricted]])
(GET "/just-for'you" [] (restricted (render-private-page)))
```

Alternatively, we can restrict access to multiple routes by using the `def-restricted-routes` macro. The `def-restricted-routes` macro is exactly like the `defroutes` macro we've been using in the various `hipstr.routes.*` namespaces, with the exception that it will mark all defined routes as `restricted` on our behalf. For example, instead of doing something like this:

```
(defroutes ;everything here will be public,
           ;unless marked otherwise
  (GET "/" [] (render-home-page))
  (GET "/protected [] (restricted (render-protected-page)))
  (GET "/another-public" [] (render-another-public-page)))
```

We can separate our protected from our public routes:

```
(defroutes ;everything here will be public
  (GET "/" [] (render-home-page))
  (GET "/another-public" [] (render-another-public-page)))
(def-restricted-routes ;these are all protected, obviously
  (GET "/protected" [] (render-protected-page)))
```

There are pros and cons to each, but mostly from a route management perspective. If your application is small and you only have a handful of routes, or if all of your protected routes are under a specific URI, then it probably makes sense to just use the `restricted` macro directly. However, if you have dozens or hundreds of routes spread about several pages, then it may make sense to make use of the `def-protected-routes` macro; however, that also comes at the cost of doubling the number of routes you have to import in your handler. It's give and take. Frankly, I've never worked on a project that's grown quite so large wherein we didn't have to refactor our routes at least once, so whichever strategy you choose may change over time.

So we now know how to restrict routes, but how do we access them? How does Luminus know that the requester of the route is okay to access the route?

# Accessing a restricted route

Rules governing restricted routes are subjective. Every application, and in fact many routes within the same application, may have different rules governing access. Luminus allows us to define each of these rules to varying layers of granularity by using the `:access-rules` key of the `app-handler`, which hipstr makes use of when defining `hipstr.handler/app`:

```
(def app (app-handler
  ;...snipped for brevity
  ;; add access rules here
  :access-rules []
  ;…snipped for brevity
  )
```

By default, the `:access-rules` are empty. An empty `:access-rules` is basically a skeleton key, unlocking every restricted door in the house. In our `just-for-you` example, the `restricted` macro won't actually do anything because we've yet to define an access rule. There are two ways we can define an access rule, either as a function, or as a map.

# Access rule as a function

Access rule functions accept a request map and return a value. If the returned value is *truthy*, then access will be granted, otherwise the user will be redirected to /. With that in mind, we could create a simple and completely useless access rule such as the following:

```
:access-rules [#(-> (java.util.UUID/randomUUID) str keyword %)]
```

In the preceding code, we're generating a random UUID, getting its string representation, turning it into a keyword, and, finally, checking to see if that keyword is in the request map (which it won't be because UUIDs are, by definition, guaranteed to be universally unique). Since the access rule always returns false, and it's the only access rule we've defined, all requests to a route marked as restricted will redirect the user to /.

If we changed the rule to return true under certain circumstances, say, if a particular value is in the session, then the the request will be granted access to any restricted route.

Access rules as a function don't provide us with many options, as it's basically a *one-ring-to-rule-them-all* approach; we can't even define where to redirect the user if access is not granted. This may be fine if you're designing a REST API that requires an authentication token. However, for a web application with human interaction, it's not the best. For this reason, it's likely that you'll define access rules as a map.

# Access rule as a map

Defining an access rule as a map opens the door for customization. While a rule as a map still requires us to write at least 1 rule function, we can also define different rules for different routes, redirect to different URIs, and define what to do in case of a failed attempt (instead of just redirecting the user – such as returning a 403 response in a REST API instead of a 302 Redirect). We can even have multiple rule functions for a single access rule and state whether we want any or all of the rules to pass in order for access to be granted.

The map equivalent of our access-rule-as-a-function example would look like the following:

```
:access-rules [{:rule
  #(-> (java.util.UUID/randomUUID) str keyword %)}]
```

This looks roughly the same, but with a bit more noise, thus calling into question why we would define it as such. However, we could do something like the following:

```
:access-rules [{:uri "/just-for-you"
                :rule #(->(java.utiul.UUID/randomUUID)
str keyword %)
                :redirect "/access-denied"}]
```

Ah, now we're getting somewhere. Instead of redirecting the user to / (the default), the preceding access rule will redirect the user to /access-denied because we defined a value for :redirect. Also, by specifying the :uri keyword, the rule will only be applied to that URI instead of all URIs. Alternatively, we can use :uris to define multiple URIs against which the :rule will be applied:

```
:access-rules [{:uris ["/just-for-you" "/and-maybe-you"]…}]
```

However, in the preceding case, the route will still always redirect the user to /access-denied because our rule will always return false. We can, however, provide multiple rules and specify if *any* of them match to grant access:

```
:access-rules [{:rules {:any [
                #(->(java.utiul.UUID/randomUUID) str keyword %)
                #(= (:username %) "TheDude")]}…}]
```

In the preceding example, the access rule will grant access if either the first UUID function returns true (which it never will,) or if the request map has the :username of TheDude. Alternatively, by using :all instead of :any, all of the rules would have to return *truthy* in order for the access rule to be satisfied.

> Please note, dear reader, that this is just a trivial example to understand what we can do. Your access rules will likely (please?) be more complex and secure than something so easily *spoofable*. But you knew that already.

Finally, if we didn't want to return a 302 redirect to some URI on failure, we can use the :on-fail key to specify what to do as a response. For example, we could, instead, render a basic 403 Unauthorized page:

```
(require '[noir.util.response :as response])
:access-rules [{:on-fail (fn [req]
                (response/status
                  (response/response "Unauthorized") 403))…}]
```

Defining access rules as maps provides granularity and flexibility for authorization within our application, while keeping the syntax relatively low. It's easy to get our head around it all, and simple to expand.

# Cookies

Show me a website without any cookies, and I'll show you a pamphlet. At some point, you're going to need to write a cookie. Indeed, we've already seen that Ring writes out a cookie for us right out of the box for session tracking.

We can interact with cookies using the `noir.cookies` namespace. At its most basic, `noir.cookies` provides two functions: `get` and `put!`.

## Getting a cookie's value

We can get a cookie's value by calling `noir.cookies/get` and providing either a string or a keyword for the name of the cookie to retrieve. We can see this in action by creating a trivial route that simply renders out the value of the ring-session cookie:

```
(require '[compojure.core :refer :all]
         '[noir.cookies :as cookies])
(defroutes some-route
  (GET "/ring-session" [] (cookies/get "ring-session"))    ;#1
```

The call to `cookies/get` retrieves the value of the cookie in question – if one exists – otherwise `nil`. In our case, the preceding code would render something similar to the following:

# Setting a cookie's value

Knowing how to read a cookie's value is all fine and dandy, but it's about as useless as wearing a raincoat indoors if we don't know how to write a value to a cookie in the first place. We accomplish this by calling `noir.cookies/put!`, and, similar to `get`, pass it either as a string or a keyword for the name of the cookie. You can write the cookie from any code that's executed during the processing of the route, though I typically write out my cookies as close to the route def as possible. For example:

```
(require '[noir.cookies :as cookies])
(defn write-cookie-page
  "Just writes a cookie and a friendly message to the browser."
  []
  (cookies/put! :my-cookie "om nom nom nom!")
  "Hey there, buddy ol' chap!")
(defroutes some-routes
  (GET "/write-cookie" [] (write-cookie-page)))
```

The preceding code simply writes out a cookie, called my-cookie, with the value of `"om nom nom nom!"`. All the other settings are left with their default values.

Similar to access rules, if we only provide a string as the value of a cookie, then a reasonable set of defaults will be used for the cookie (such as max-age, expires, path, domain, and so on). If we want to be specific about the cookie attributes however, we can set the cookie's value as a map.

## Setting the cookie as a map

Setting the cookie as a map, as opposed to a string value, provides us with more granularity of how the cookie behaves. The cookie-as-a-map representation of the preceding example would be the following:

```
(cookies/put! :my-cookie {:value "om nom nom nom!"})
```

Other values we can specify in the map are:

- `:path` (string): This is the URI on which the cookie is valid. Defaults to /
- `:domain` (string): This is the domain on which the cookie is valid. Defaults to the current domain
- `:port` (int): This is the port on which the cookie is valid.
- `:max-age` (int): This is the number of seconds the cookie is valid for, after which, it expires

- :expires (string): Instead of the number seconds, a date-time string explicitly stating when the cookie will expire

- :secure (Boolean): A true/false value which, when true, states that the cookie requires HTTPS access

- :http-only (Boolean): A true/false value which, when true, prohibits JavaScript from accessing the cookie

I will fully admit that I've never used the :domain or :port options, and I rarely use :expires because I almost never have a need to specify a specific date (the number of seconds usually suffices, and it's easier to set than messing around with date math). But I digress...

If we wanted to set up the precedingly mentioned cookie such that it was only available on our login page, and only over HTTPS, and not available to JavaScript, we could adjust it to the following:

```
(cookies/put! :my-cookie
                    {:value "om nom nom nom!"
                     :path "/login"
                     :secure true
                     :http-only true})
```

# Securing a cookie

In addition to the standard get/put! functions for reading and writing a cookie, we can also use two other functions that will *securely* read and write a cookie: get-signed and put-signed!:

- put-signed!: This writes a second cookie alongside the original cookie, containing a signature for the cookie. The signature cookie's name is the same as the original cookie, but with the suffix __s.

- get-signed: This validates the signature of the cookie that was created using put-signed!

Note that put-signed! doesn't encrypt the cookie; rather, it writes a second cookie containing a signature for the first. As such, you can write a cookie using put-signed!, but can still read it using get. The validation of the cookie's signature is only performed when reading the cookie using get-signed, which, if invalid, nil will be returned instead of the cookie's value.

Beware! If you use `put-signed!` to write a cookie, and then later change the cookie's value using just `put!`, the signature cookie will not be updated; thus any subsequent `get-signed` will fail to validate the cookie.

# Deleting a cookie

This is probably the most commonly asked question on the Internet when it comes to cookies, so I figured I would include it here. In short, there is no way to delete a cookie. The best way to *delete* a cookie is to overwrite the cookie with an empty value, and then set its `:max-age` to `-1` (one second in the past).

We could delete our `:my-cookie` cookie then by overwriting it with the following code:

```
(cookies/put! :my-cookie {:value "" :max-age -1})
```

Note, however, that this only deletes the `:my-cookie` cookie and not its accompanying signature cookie, `:my-cookie__s`, which will also need to be overwritten if you wish to *delete* it.

# Extending the application: brief requirements

With that, it's time to put it all in practice and extend our application. The requirements for this extension are simple. We want to:

1. Restrict the `/albums/recently-added` routes (both the GET and POST) to only authenticated users.

2. We want to give the user the option for us to remember their username for future authentications.

3. We want to have a logout link that kills the user's session, and then prohibits them from gaining access to restricted routes until they re-authenticate.

If we break this down, there are a few work items for us. We need to create a login form that we'll use to get the user's credentials to authenticate, which should take the place of item 1. We can also satisfy item 2 by putting a classic *Remember my username* checkbox on the authentication form as well. Finally, we'll need to put a logout link somewhere on our site. No problemo! Let's get cracking!

# Creating the login form

We're going to build the login form first because, hey, we need to get the credentials somehow and a phone call isn't going to cut it. For now, it's probably easiest if we just create the login Selmer template next to the signup form template we created in *Chapter 7, Getting Started with the Database*. We can do the following:

1.  Create a new file, `resources/templates/login.html`.

2.  Fill the file with the following:

```
{% extends "templates/base.html" %}   <!-- 1 -->
{% block content %}
<h1>Login. <span class="small">That last session was so lame.</
span></h1>
<div class="row">
  <div class="col-md-6">
    {% if invalid-credentials? %}   <!-- 2 -->
    <p class="errors">The provided username and/or
    password are incorrect.
    </p>
    {% endif %}
    <form role="form" method="POST" action="/login">
      <div class="form-group">
        <label for="username">Username</label>
        <input type="text" name="username"
          class="form-control" id="username"
          placeholder="AtticusButch">
      </div>
      <div class="form-group">
        <label for="password">Password</label>
        <input type="password" name="password"
          class="form-control" id="password">
      </div>
      <div class="form-group">
      </div>
      <button type="submit"
        class="btn btn-default">Submit</button>
    </form>
  </div>
</div>
{% endblock %}
```

The form looks pretty similar to our signup form. We're extending our base template (at <!-- 1 -->), and we have a username and password field that we'll be POSTing to /login. The last thing we're doing is conditionally rendering a *Wrong username/ password* message if the :invalid-credentials? key is on the context (<!-- 2 -->).

Of course we need to be able to render this form, so let's create a new route for the /login URI. The /signup route is handled in the hipstr.routes.home namespace, so we'll put the /login route there as well. In the hipstr.routes.home namespace, do the following:

1. Add a route to the home-routes that manages the GET method for /login:

   ```
   (GET "/login" [] (login-page))
   ```

2. Add the hipstr.routes.home/login-page route helper function. This will simply render the login page:

   ```
   (defn login-page
     "Renders the login form."
     []
     (layout/render "login.html"))
   ```

That should be all there is to it. We can now fire up a browser and navigate to http://localhost:3000/login, and we should see something similar to the following:

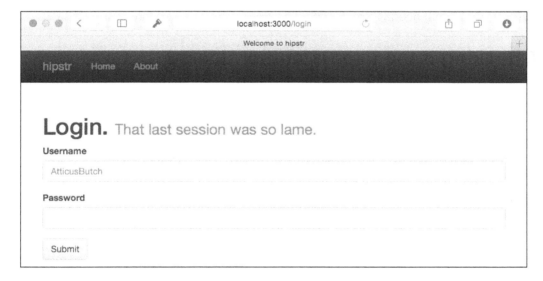

Next, let's lock down the /albums/recently-added routes.

# Restricting the recently-added route

As we saw earlier in the chapter, restricting access to routes is a two-step process. We need to A, mark the route as `restricted`, and B, tell Luminus how to grant a access to the restricted route. Let's first restrict the route.

## Restricting the route

In the `hipstr.routes.albums` namespace, add the following requirement:

```
(:require …
          [noir.util.route :refer [restricted]])
```

This imports the `restricted` macro that we'll use to restrict access to the 2 routes in question. To do this, we'll modify the GET and POST routes for `/albums/recently-added` as `restricted`:

```
(defroutes album-routes
  (GET "/albums/recently-added" [] (restricted (recently-added-page)))
  (POST "/albums/recently-added" [& album-form]
    (restricted (recently-added-submit album-form)))
  …
```

That's all there is to restricting access to a route, as far as the route is concerned. However, now we have to tell Luminus when *not* to restrict access to the route. And for that, we'll need to create a new access rule in our app handler.

## Checking if the user is authenticated

I typically like to keep things partitioned a bit. We need to put some code somewhere that checks if a user is authenticated. For now the most natural place for that is in our `hipstr.models.user-model` namespace (or someplace else, if you prefer).

Let's create the `hipstr.models.user-model/is-authed?` function first, to check if a request is authenticated. This function will simply check if there's a `:user_id` in the session for the current request.

First, bring the `noir.session` into the `hipstr.models.user-model` namespace:

```
…
(:require …
          [noir.session :as session]
…)
```

Secondly, add the following function to `hipstr.models.user-model`:

```
(defn is-authed?
  "Returns false if the current request is anonymous; otherwise
  true."
  [_] ;#1
  (not (nil? (session/get :user_id))))
```

The substance of this function is simple. The only thing to note is that we don't care about the parameter (#1). Every access rule is passed the request map, but we're more concerned about the session, so we just ignore it.

## Defining the access rule

The last thing we need to do is define the access rule. We know that, if our application were to grow big and strong, we may define several access rules governing various routes. So, instead of cluttering up the `hipstr.handler` namespace, we'll create a new `hipstr.routes.access` namespace and define our rules there.

1. Create a new namespace, `hipstr.routes.access`, and give it access to our new `is-authed?` function:

   ```
   (ns hipstr.routes.access
     (:require [hipstr.models.user-model :refer [is-authed?]]))
   ```

2. Create a def called `rules` that returns a vector of access-rule maps. Our vector will only contain a single rule, which defers validation to the `is-authed?` function:

   ```
   (def rules
     "The rules for accessing various routes in our application."
     [{:redirect "/login" :rule is-authed?}])
   ```

3. Finally, in our `hipstr.handler/app` application handler, set our `:access-rules` to the rules vector we just defined:

   ```
   (def app (app-handler
              ...
              :access-rules access/rules
              ...))
   ```

 Don't forget to `:require` the `hipstr.access` namespace at the top!

With that, any anonymous request to a restricted route will automatically be redirected to the /login route, where our gorgeous login form will be presented to the user. We can test our route restriction by trying to navigate directly to http://localhost:3000/albums/recently-added, which should automatically redirect us to /login.

 If the access rule fails to redirect you, try restarting the Ring Server and then hitting the restricted route again.

Now that we have a restricted route and a login form, let's move on to authenticating the user.

# Authenticating the user

The form POST will do 3 things. First, it will try and validate the user's credentials. There's no need for us to validate the format of the credentials coming up the pipe, because we already ensured they're in the appropriate format when we put them in the database as part of our Signup page. So the credentials on the login form will either match something in the database or they won't. Secondly, if the set of credentials fail to validate, then we'll re-render the login page and tell the user that their username/password was incorrect (that is, make use of that `invalid-credentials` context value the form is currently expecting). Finally, if the credentials successfully validate, we'll redirect the user to the /albums/recently-added route we had previously locked down.

## Validating the credentials

Since our `hipstr.models.user-model` has the `is-authed?` function, it makes sense to put an `auth-user` function beside it. The function will grab a user from the database matching the provided `username` and, if it exists, will check if the passwords match. However, you'll recall in *Chapter 7, Getting Started with the Database* that we store a hashed version of the password, so we'll need to make use of the `crypto.password.bcrypt` namespace (the same namespace we used to originally hash the password for storage). If the username and password match, we'll return the user map from the database; otherwise we'll return `nil` (including if a user with the provided username does not exist).

First, we'll need to create a simple SQL query that fetches a user by username. Add the following in our `users.sql` file:

```
-- name: get-user-by-username
-- Fetches a user from the DB based on username.
SELECT *
FROM users
WHERE username=:username
```

The preceding query will be processed by YeSQL at runtime, resulting in a `get-user-by-username` function in our namespace. Next, add the following function to the `hipstr.models.user-model`:

```
(defn auth-user
  "Validates a username/password and, if they match, adds the
  user_id to the session and returns the user map from
  the database. Otherwise nil."
  [username password]
  (let [user (first (get-user-by-username
                      {:username username}))]        ;#1
    (when (and user (password/check password
                      (:password user)))             ;#2
      (session/put! :user_id (:user_id user))        ;#3
      (dissoc user :password))))                     ;#4
```

The `auth-user` function makes use of the YeSQL-generated `get-user-by-username` function (#1), which, if successful, will return a map of matching users. Since our `users.username` database field has a unique index constraint on it, we know that only 0 or 1 result will be returned in the vector, hence the call to `first`. We then make use of the `crypto.password.bcrypt/check` function (#2), which returns true if the hashed password matches an unhashed password. If the user exists and the passwords match, we then stuff the `:user_id` into the session (#3), and then return the user map – but without the password (#4), as there's no need to proliferate that throughout our app.

If all is happy, then the `:user_id` will be added to the user's session, which is what our access rule checks for all restricted routes. The last thing we need to do to authenticate the user is to handle that pesky form POST.

# Handling the form POST

We'll overload the `hipstr.routes.home/login-page` to accept a different arity of arguments, specifically the login form's value map. Extend it to the following:

```
(defn login-page
  ([]
    (layout/render "login.html" {:username (cookies/remember-me)}))
  ([credentials]
    (if (apply u/auth-user (map credentials [:username :password]))
      (response/redirect "/albums/recently-added"))
      (layout/render "login.html" {:invalid-credentials? true}))))
```

The overloaded function is pretty simple: If the user successfully authenticates with the username and password, then redirect them to the restricted route / albums/recently-added. Otherwise, re-render the login form with the invalid-credentials set to true. The last thing to do before we try out the login form is to create the POST /login route. Add the following to the home-routes:

```
(POST "/login" [& login-form] (login-page login-form))
```

Try it out for yourself! If we provide an incorrect username or password, our login form is re-rendered with a foreboding blood-red error message:

And when we provide a valid username/password, we're redirected to the /
albums/recently-added page:

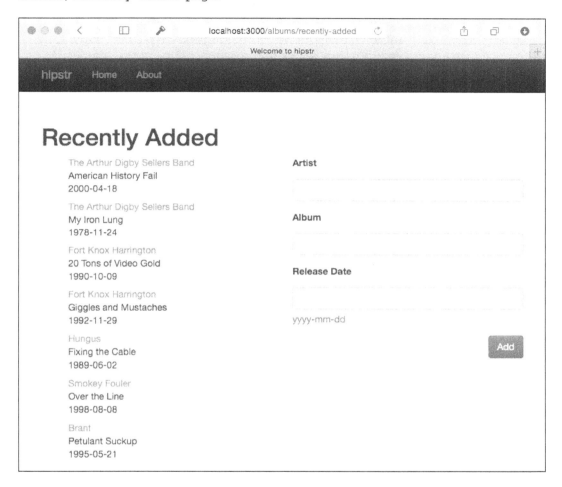

But typing in our username is so boring! I have a thousand websites and a thousand
usernames, so let's take care of action item number 2 in our requirements and add
that *remember me* cookie.

# Writing the "Remember Me" cookie

Over the years, I've become rather disdainful of random cookie code littered throughout a web application. I prefer to keep cookies in a rather central location. That way, when we want to change the way a cookie behaves we only have to do it once instead of a gazillion times. For that reason, create another namespace, `hipstr.cookies`, and throw the following in there:

```
(ns hipstr.cookies
  (:require [noir.cookies :as c]))

(defn remember-me
  ([]
    "Gets the username in the remember-me cookie."
    (c/get :remember-me))
  ([username]
    "Sets a remember-me cookie to the user's browser with the
user's username."
    (if username
      (c/put! :remember-me {:value username
                            :path "/"
                            :max-age (* 60 60 24 365)})
      (c/put! :remember-me {:value "" :path "/" :max-age -1}))))
```

The `hisptr.cookies` acts as a kind of business wrapper to the `noir.cookies` namespace. In this namespace, we put an overloaded `remember-me` function, which will either get or set the value of the `remember-me` cookie, depending on whether or not it's called with a value. You'll notice in the overloaded function that, if we call remember-me with a *falsey* value (`nil` or `""`) that we'll basically *delete* the cookie.

To make use of the `remember-me` cookie, let's extend our login form to include a simple checkbox. Back in the `resources/templates/login.html`, add the following between the password field and the submit button:

```
<div class="form-group">
  <label for="password">Password</label>
  <input type="password" name="password" class="form-control"
id="password">
</div>
<div class="form-group">
  <input type="checkbox" name="remember-me"
```

```
  {% if username %} checked{% endif %}>
  Remember me on this computer
</div>
<button type="submit" class="btn btn-default">Submit</button>
```

All we did here was add a simple HTML checkbox. Yep. Living on the edge! The checkbox will now be marked `checked` if there's a `username` on the context map. Let's also set the value of the `username` text field to the `username` context value:

```
<input type="text" name="username" class="form-control"
id="username" placeholder="AtticusButch" value="{{ username }}">
```

Next we'll modify our `hipstr.routes.home/login-page` to take the `remember-me` cookie and checkbox into account. First, import the `hipstr.cookies` namespace:

```
(:require …
          [hipstr.cookies :as cookies]
          …)
```

Next, we'll set the `username` context value when rendering the login page:

```
([]
(layout/render "login.html" {:username (cookies/remember-me)})
```

Finally, if the user has checked the remember-me checkbox, and they successfully authenticate on POST, we'll write their username to the `remember-me` cookie, otherwise we'll set the cookie to `nil` (essentially deleting it):

```
(if (apply u/auth-user (map credentials [:username :password]))
  (do (if (:remember-me credentials)
        (cookies/remember-me (:username credentials))
        (cookies/remember-me ""))
    (response/redirect "/albums/recently-added")))
```

With all that, we should now see a checkbox on the login form. The first time we view it, it will be unchecked. However, if we check it and successfully authenticate, and then go back to the login form, you'll notice that it will be checked and our username will be pre-populated in the username text field, shown as follows:

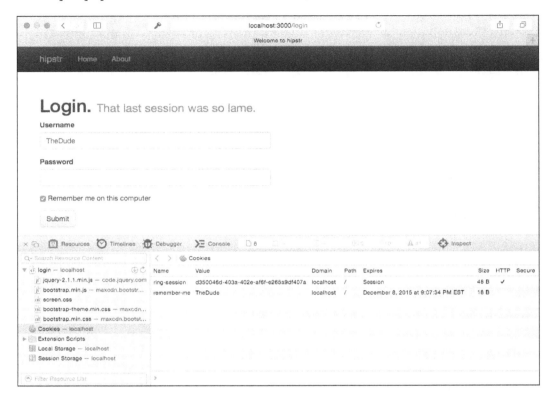

Finally, the last thing we need to do is create the logout route and link to it.

# Creating the logout route

Our logout link will be simple. Any form of navigation (GET, POST, etc.) to `/logout` will invalidate the user's authenticated status and redirect back to `/`. Since our `is-authed?` and `auth-user` functions are in `hisptr.models.user-model`, we will add a third method alongside them, called `invalidate-auth`:

```
(defn invalidate-auth
  "Invalidates a user's current authenticated state."
  []
  (session/clear!))
```

That's it. We'll just blow away anything in the session because, hey, why not! Technically, if all we wanted to do was prohibit the user from accessing restricted routes, we could have simply called (session/remove! :user_id), and that would have sufficed. But for now, there are no business rules keeping us from blowing everything away – also, it frees up some memory.

Next, we'll add the route and the helper function. Add the following function and route to our hipstr.routes.home namespace:

```
(defn logout []
  "Logs the user out of this session."
  (u/invalidate-auth)
  (response/redirect "/"))

(defroutes home-routes
  ...
  (ANY "/logout" [] (logout))
  ...)
```

Finally, we need to get a **Logout** link in there. Since we're extending base.html for all of our templates, that seems like the best place to put it. This allows us to put the logout link in the top-right corner of every page. Open the templates/base.html file and append the following highlighted markup (roughly line 19):

```
<div class="navbar-collapse collapse ">
  <ul class="nav navbar-nav">
    <li class="{{home-selected}}">
      <a href="{{servlet-context}}/">Home</a></li>
    <li class="{{about-selected}}">
    <a href="{{servlet-context}}/about">About</a></li>
  </ul>
  <ul class="nav navbar-nav navbar-right">
    <li><a href="{{servlet-context}}/logout">Logout</a></li>
  </ul>
</div>
```

Save the file and refresh your browser, and you'll now see a **Logout** link in the top-right corner of your browser:

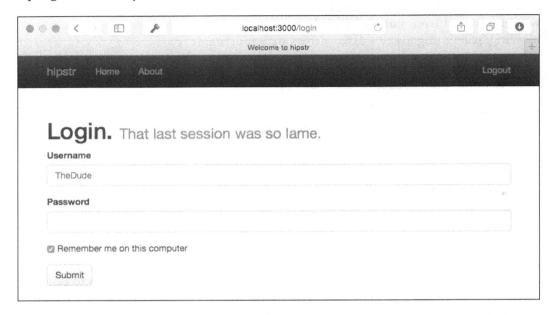

There's only one problem though: A link saying **Logout** doesn't make a lot of sense if you're not already authenticated. so change the code to the following:

```
<ul class="nav navbar-nav navbar-right">
  {% if is-authed? %}
    <li><a href="{{servlet-context}}/logout">Logout</a></li>
  {% else %}
    <li><a href="{{servlet-context}}/login">Login</a></li>
  {% endif %}
</ul>
```

We will now render the appropriate link if the `is-authed?` context value is true. But where is that value coming from? We need to set it on the context. Considering that this link will be on every single one of our pages, it makes sense for us to adjust the `hipstr.layout/render` function. This is the function we call every time we render an HTML template. We can associate the `:is-authed?` context value with the parameter map coming in:

1. First, include the `hipstr.models.user-model` in `hipstr.layout` namespace:

```
(:require ...
          [hipstr.models.user-model :as user]
          ...)
```

2. Adjust the `render` function to associate the `is-authed?` key with the value returned by `hipstr.models.user-model/is-authed?`:

```
(defn render [template & [params]]
  (let [params (-> (or params {})
                   (assoc :is-authed? (user/is-authed? nil)))]
    (RenderableTemplate. template params)))
```

The `base.html` template will now show the appropriate Login/Logout link, depending on the user's current authenticated status.

# Summary

This chapter covered some of the fundamentals that nearly every web application requires. We learned how to interact with the session, as well as some basic session setup. We also learned how to read, write, and delete cookies, and how to create access rules to restrict access to routes. And with that, the functionality of our hipstr application is complete. In the next chapter, we'll learn how to manage configuration files, as well as how to deploy our application in a few standard ways.

# 11
# Environment Configuration and Deployment

So far, we've built a simple but fairly well-rounded application, hipstr, which performs many of the every-day tasks required by web applications. This chapter will focus on a couple different ways one can deploy a Clojure-based web application, as well as how to abstract the environment configurations that will differ from deployment to deployment. In this chapter, we will cover the following topics:

- **environ**, a library for reading environment configurations
- How to pass environment variables to our application outside our development environment
- How to deploy our application to a few common setups

By the end of this chapter, you'll know the basics of how to abstract the application's environment configuration, and how to get this thing up and running outside the Leiningen Ring Server plugin. We're almost there. Can you taste it?

## Environ

Luminus-generated applications make use of the `environ` library, which was written by James Reeves, the essential Godfather of Clojure web development (remember, this guy wrote Ring, the Ring Server, and about every other underpinning library we've used in this book). The `environ` library allows applications to read environment variables set from outside the scope of any internalized configuration. This is important to remember: `environ` accepts environment configurations only from outside the application, thus adhering to the third tenant (Configuration) of the 12 Factor-Application Pattern.

You can read more about the 12 Factor-Application Pattern at http://12factor.net. While not necessary for this chapter, it's something I encourage any software developer to read, as the practices contained within are beneficial for any software you're writing.

# Using environ

Consuming environment configuration through `environ` is trivial. Let's assume we have an environment variable called DB_USER with the value bunny. We can get the value of this environment variable by doing the following:

```
(require '[environ.core :refer [env]])
(env :db-user)
>> bunny
```

Well, that was easy. But why did we get the environment variable using the :db-user instead of DB_USER? Good question!

# Variable translations

The `environ` library is smart enough – and kind enough – to take into account typical Clojure naming conventions, as well as the naming conventions of traditional environment variables and Java system properties. As such, `environ` will *translate* the names of the variables to a more Clojure-friendly convention. The specifics are as follows:

- Underscores and periods will be converted to hyphens
- Variable names will be lower-cased
- Variable names will be turned into keywords

That's why the value of our environment variable, DB_USER, was retrieved using the keyword :db-user. Likewise, specifying a Java system property at the command line, such as -Ddb.user=bunny, will also be translated into :db-user.

# Setting and resolving environment configurations

We've already alluded to the fact that you can set configuration for `environ` to consume from either environment variables or from Java system properties. This covers about 100% of real-world usage. However, during development, we can also set environment configuration using the `lein-environ` plugin (which is also packaged as part of a Luminus-generated application).

When running the development server using `lein ring server`, the `lein-environ` plugin will fetch environment configuration from the Leiningen project map, as well as an optional `profiles.clj` file, and merge the two together into the `.lein-env` file. This `.lein-env` file is the first go-to place for environment settings, but *only* when running the development server.

> It is recommended that the `profiles.clj` and `.lein-env` files not be committed into your version control, as every developer's environment is likely to be somewhat different. Plus, despite the fact that `.lein-env` supports fetching configuration from `~/.lein/profiles.clj`, I consider that a nasty practice; an application's configuration changes from environment to environment, and configurable requirements change from application to application. So, setting what amounts to a *global* developer configuration for all applications has a pretty bad smell to it.

In the case of our `:db-user` example, we could put the following in a `profiles.clj` file located in hipstr's project folder:

```
{:dev {:env {:db-user "bunny"}}}
```

We aren't restricted to defining a single environment in the `profiles.clj` file. We can define multiple environments by doing the following:

```
{:dev {:env {:db-user "bunny"}}
 :test {:env {:db-user "test-bunny"}}}
```

We tell our development server which profile to use when we launch the development server, using the `with-profile` argument:

```
# lein with-profile dev ring server
```

The `lein ring server` command defaults to `:dev` if no `with-profile` is declared. Hence, consider the following code:

```
# lein with-profile test ring server
```

On executing the above code, our `(env :db-user)` would resolve to `test-bunny`.

# Resolving environment configuration

The `environ` library will check three different places for a matching configuration key:

- The `.lein-env` file
- Exported environment variables
- Java system properties

If the requested configuration key isn't found in `.lein-env`, then `environ` will check any exported environment variables, and, if still not found, it will check the Java system properties. If the configuration key is not found, `environ` will ultimately return `nil`.

# Adjusting the database connection

In essence, the Configuration principle of the 12 Factor-Application Pattern states that an application's configuration and an application's code should be completely independent of each other. Our hipstr application currently violates this principle in a key area: the database connection. This, however, is easily resolved.

# Creating the profiles.clj file

For our development server, we will create `profiles.clj` and have the `lein-env` plugin generate the `.lein-env` file. Currently, our `hipstr.models.connection/db-spec` expects 5 settings: `:classname`, `:subprotocol`, `:subname`, `:user`, and `:password`.

Theoretically, we could transfer the entire `db-spec` map into the `profiles.clj` file, such as shown below:

```
{:dev {:env {:db-spec {:classname   "org.postgresql.Driver"
                       :subprotocol "postgresql"
                       :subname     "//localhost/postgres"
                       :user        "hipstr"
                       :password    "p455w0rd"})
```

We could then modify `hipstr.models.connection/db-spec` to just the following:

```
(ns hipstr.models.connection
  (:require [environ.core :refer [env]]))
(def db-spec (env :db-spec))
```

However, this would prove to be our fall from grace during deployment outside the development server, because `environ` does not support embedded configuration maps for environment variables or Java system properties. As such, we need to flatten our settings. So do the following steps:

1. Create a new `profiles.clj` file alongside our `project.clj` file in the hipstr project folder.

2. Add the following map:

```
{:dev {:env {:dev? true
       :db-classname  "org.postgresql.Driver"
       :db-subprotocol "postgresql"
       :db-subname     "//localhost/postgres"
       :db-user             "hipstr"
       :db-password     "p455w0rd"}}}
```

The next time you run `lein ring server`, the `.lein-env` file will be generated and the above `profiles.clj` map will be included, thus allowing `environ` to find the settings when called upon.

# Modifying the hipstr.models.connection namespace

Next, we need to modify our `hipstr.models.connection` namespace to make use of the `environ` library:

1. Adjust the `hipstr.models.connection` namespace to include `environ`:

```
(ns hipstr.models.connection
  (:require [environ.core :refer [env]]))
```

2. Next, simply replace each hardcoded database configuration value with the `environ` equivalent:

```
(def db-spec {:classname    (env :db-classname)
              :subprotocol  (env :db-subprotocol)
              :subname      (env :db-subname)
              :user         (env :db-user)
              :password     (env :db-password)})
```

That's all we have to do! Our database connection can now read configuration from anywhere `environ` resolves the key!

Before we restart our development server however, let's adjust the `migratus-config` in the `hipstr.handler` namespace. In the `hipstr.handler` namespace, perform the following steps:

1. Add a reference to our `hipstr.models.connection/db-spec` in the `:require`:

```
(ns hipstr.handler
  (:require [compojure.core :refer [defroutes]]
            [hipstr.models.connection :refer [db-spec]]
            ...)
```

2. Remove the hardcoded `:db` map in our `migratus-config`, and instead use the referred `db-spec`:

```
(def migratus-config
  {:store :database
   :migration-dir "migrations"
   :migration-table-name "_migrations"
   :db db-spec})
```

That's it! All of our database references are now using an external configuration. Restart your development server and create a new user, and you'll find that everything behaves the same way.

# Deploying the hipstr application

The `lein-ring` plugin can create 2 different types of packages for deployment: an `uberjar` or an `uberwar`. These are created using `lein ring uberjar` or `lein ring uberwar` respectively:

- **uberjar**: Creates an executable `.jar` file containing all dependencies, including an embedded Jetty server

- **uberwar**: Creates a standard `.war` file containing all dependencies, which can be deployed to any Java web application server (such as **Tomcat** or **GlassFish**)

 Check out the official *lein-ring* documentation to get more details about the various options available for `ring uberwar/uberjar` at `https://github.com/weavejester/lein-ring`.

How you're going to deploy your application determines how you're going to package your application.

# When to use an uberjar

Because Ring applications have an embedded Jetty server, we have the option of creating a self-contained, fully independent uberjar, which contains all the required dependencies and can run on its own. The advantage of this is that deployment becomes dead simple – you simply copy the uberjar to a server and run it as you would any other Java application (we'll do this later in the chapter). If we want another instance of our app, we can simply fire it up like any other Java app – Ring will automatically determine which port to serve on (starting at 3000 and going up from there).

Running as an uberjar has some drawbacks though: You don't get a fancy administrative console like you do with a Java application server, which means that you'll be rolling a lot of configuration by hand. The standalone uberjar is pretty barebones, but in the world of web applications, rarely have I worked on anything that actually required all the functionality that's embedded inside an application server.

# When to use an uberwar

If you plan on deploying to an application server, then you'll need to package the application as an uberwar.

Application servers provide a whole truckload of features, such as queuing, configuration management, clustering (though we can use **Nginx** and multiple instances of a standalone server to accomplish this), and so on. Most application servers allow you to configure their features through a UI (though in my experience these are often clunky). Some application servers, such as GlassFish, are free and open source. Others, however, such as WebSphere and WebLogic, cost an arm and a leg.

The downsides of application servers are cost and, often times, bloated. They can be fairly resource intensive, expensive, and complicated. Also, chances are you aren't going to need an application server; in the world of Clojure web application development, I've yet to write anything that requires the golden handcuffs of an application server. Most Clojure web applications are deployed as a standalone application.

# Deploying as a standalone

The easiest way to deploy a Ring application is as a standalone application, and just use the embedded Jetty server. This is the killer feature as far as I'm concerned. To create a standalone hipstr application, perform the following steps:

1. In a terminal, and from the project root folder, run `lein ring uberjar`. This produces 2 jars:

   ° `./target/hipstr-0.1.0-SNAPSHOT.jar`: Contains all our hipstr application code and dependencies.

   ° `./target/hipstr-0.1.0-SNAPSHOT-standalone.jar`: An executable, standalone version which includes an embedded Jetty server and all dependencies. This is entirely self-contained.

2. Fire up the hipstr application by doing the following in the `./target` directory (keeping in mind that we can use Java system properties to set the environment configuration, such as the `-D` Java system properties below):

```
# java -jar -Ddb.classname=org.postgresql.Driver -Ddb.
subprotocol=postgresql -Ddb.subname=//localhost/postgres -Ddb.
user=hipstr -Ddb.password=p455w0rd hipstr-0.1.0-SNAPSHOT-
standalone.jar
```

 If you get an error about "could not find `users.sql`", ensure the `[:uberjar :omit-source]` in `project.clj` file is set to false. If set to `true`, then `lein ring uberjar` will remove our `.sql` files from the packaged jar.

As is the case with the development server, the above command will serve on port 3000. Also like the development server, the above command will execute in the foreground, which you can stop by hitting *Ctrl + C*, or by shutting down the terminal. *However*, in a non-dev/local environment you'll want to run the application in the background, which can be done by using `nohup`:

```
# nohup java -jar -Ddb.classname=org.postgresql.Driver -Ddb.
subprotocol=postgresql -Ddb.subname=//localhost/postgres -Ddb.
user=hipstr -Ddb.password=p455w0rd hipstr-0.1.0-SNAPSHOT-standalone.
jar &
```

This will persist the application after you close down the terminal. To stop the application, you first get the process ID using `ps -ef`, and then `kill -15` that process:

```
# ps -ef | grep hipstr
>> 501 68443 58530   0  6:07pm ttys000 0:09.00 /usr/bin/java -jar...
# kill -15 68443
```

Keep in mind that you can export environment variables (using "_" instead of ".", such as using DB_CLASSNAME instead of db.classname) if you don't want to use Java system properties. However, this will force every instance of the hisptr application on that machine to have the same database connection. You'll have to decide which makes more sense.

# Running the application behind Nginx

Nginx is quickly becoming a popular web-server/reverse-proxy. Its configuration is relatively simple and clean compared to the now-dated Apache. And it's fast. Blisteringly fast. Scary fast!

We can use Nginx to reverse-proxy port 80 to our hipstr application's port 3000 by performing the following steps:

1. Download and install Nginx for your platform. You can download Nginx from http://wiki.nginx.org/Install.

2. Deploy and run a standalone hipstr, as outlined in the *Deploying as a standalone* section earlier in this chapter.

3. Back up the Nginx default site configuration (note that your location may differ):

   ```
   # mv /etc/nginx/sites-available/default /etc/nginx/sites-available/default.bak
   ```

4. Create a new default site configuration file with whatever your favorite tool is (I tend to use nano because I've never bothered to learn vi. Blasphemy, I know):

   ```
   # nano /etc/nginx/sites-available/default
   ```

5. Add the following configuration to the new default configuration file, specifying values for anything [inside square brackets], except the [::] wildcard:

   ```
   server {
       # listen on port 80, but apply this explicitly to
       # only the default server
         listen 80 default_server;

       # only allow IPv6 socket to process
       # IPv6 connections
         listen [::] 80 default_server ipv6only=on;

       # specify a "catch-all"; any host name on port 80
   ```

```
        # will be affected.
        server_name _;

    # log files
        access_log /var/log/hipstr_access.log;
        error_log /var/log/hipstr_error.log;

  # proxy settings
        location / {
            # proxies all requests under "/" to
            # our hipstr standalone instance
            proxy_pass http://localhost:3000/;

            # forwards the original Host header
            proxy_set_header Host $http_host;

            # forwards the X-Forwarded-For client
            # request header, if it exist,
            # as well as the client's remote
            # address (IP), separated by a comma.
            proxy_set_header X-Forwarded-For
            $proxy_add_x_forwarded_for;

            # forwards the original protocol
            # (eg. https or http)
            # in the real world you'd likely want
            # to do SSL termination, and setup
            # whatever's hosting the hipstr
            # standalone to only trust incoming
            # traffic from the fronting nginx's
            # IP.
            proxy_set_header X-Forwarded-Proto $scheme;

            # cancel the effect of all
            # proxy_redirect directives
            proxy_redirect off;
            }
    }
```

6. Reload Nginx.

```
# nginx -s reload;
```

Now whenever you hit up port 80, instead of explicitly stating port 3000, you'll get our hipstr application.

# Load balancing behind Nginx

Using Nginx, we can easily proxy multiple hipstr applications by employing a round-robin approach between all of them:

1. Open `/etc/nginx/sites-available/default` to edit it.

2. Before the `server {...}` block, add the following:

```
upstream hipstr {
    server localhost:3000;
    server localhost:3001;
    server localhost:3002;
}
```

3. Lastly, adjust `proxy_pass` in the `location /` configuration section of the `server` block so that it looks like the following:

```
location / {
    # proxies all requests under "/" to
    # our hipstr standalone instance
        proxy_pass http://hipstr;
```

4. Save and close the configuration file, then reload Nginx:

```
# nginx -s reload
```

5. Now fire up a couple more instances of the hipstr application using the `nohup` command.

That's all there is to it! You are now running a round-robin balanced cluster of hipstr applications! How easy was that!

# Summary

In this chapter, we learned how easy it is to abstract our application's configuration away from our application code. We then demonstrated how we can serve our application as a standalone app, using the embedded Jetty server. We also learned how to package an uberwar in case we wanted to deploy to a Java application server, such as GlassFish.

At this point, you have enough knowledge to be able to start writing web applications using Clojure. Did we cover everything? No, but that's why the book isn't 700 pages. However, what we did cover are the essentials, and, anything else from this point forward you should be able to learn while hitting a pint of beer and flicking through web pages on your phone. So go out and write, my friend, and bring peace and joy into this world!

# Using Korma – a Clojure DSL for SQL

In this book, we exclusively made use of YeSQL, a library that generates Clojure functions from native SQL. For an example application as small and simple as hipstr, YeSQL might be a tad overkill – its real beauty and elegance comes to light in larger projects that make use of large queries or lots of underlying database functionality. Furthermore, YeSQL does a decent job of abstracting away the underlying data model from the Clojure code.

That being said, there are many people who prefer using a domain specific language to interact with the database. This appendix will introduce you to **Korma**, a pure-Clojure DSL for SQL. This appendix will not cover Korma in its entirety (it's pretty full-fledged). Instead, this appendix will cover the following:

- How to tie object models back to database tables
- A light overview of selecting and inserting data using Korma
- Port the connection, `album-model`, and `user-model` namespaces from YeSQL to Korma

## Getting Korma

Add the following code to the Leiningen `:dependencies` in the hipstr project file:

```
[korma "0.4.0"]
```

At the time of writing this book, Version 0.4.0 is the most recent stable build of Korma, and it was released around late August of 2014. You may want to check if there's a newer version at `https://github.com/korma/Korma/`.

# The Quick Korma Crash Course

This is the ultra quick and dirty guide to Korma. We'll use the existing artists and albums tables in the hipstr database, between which a simple 1-artist-to-many-albums relationship exists:

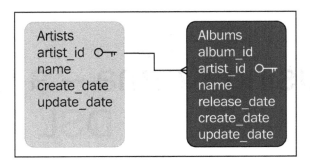

We'll gloss over just enough to make use of Korma for these two tables and how they relate to one another in the database. You can get a far more detailed and richer overview of everything Korma provides by visiting the official site at `http://www.sqlkorma.com/docs`.

## Define the database specification

You define the database Korma will use by using the `korma.db/defdb` macro. The `defdb` macro accepts a standard JDBC database map, similar to the one we created in the `hipstr.models.connection` namespace:

```
(defdb hipstr-db {:classname   "org.postgresql.Driver"
                  :subprotocol "postgresql"
                  :subname     "//localhost/postgres"
                  :user        "hipstr"
                  :password    "p455w0rd"}
```

This defines the database specification for our local hipstr database. By default, all Korma entities, unless otherwise stated, will use the most recently defined `defdb`.

## Korma entities

An **entity** is a Korma representation of a database table. Each database table we want to interact with will be done so through an entity. Picture an entity as being an object version of a database table.

An entity is defined by using the `defentity` macro. By default, the name of the entity maps to the table. So, in our case, the `artists` and `albums` tables would each have the following `defentity` declarations:

```
(use 'korma.core)
(defentity artists)
(defentity albums)
```

The preceding explanation is the most basic definition of entities, and it makes some assumptions, which we'll override later on.

# Defining the primary key

Korma assumes that the primary key for the entity is mapped to either an `id` or `[entityname]_id` column on the table. However, our tables do not conform to that assumption, as our primary keys are `artists.artist_id` and `albums.album_id` respectively. We can override the default primary keys using `korma.core`'s `pk` function:

```
(defentity artists
  (pk :artist_id))
(defentity albums
  (pk :album_id))
```

# Defining relationships between entities

Korma allows us to define the one-to-many relationship between `artists` and `albums`. We do this by using the `has-many` function on the `artists` table, and the `belongs-to` function on the `albums` table:

```
(defentity artists
  (pk :artist_id)
  (has-many albums))
(defentity albums
  (pk :album_id)
  (belongs-to artists {:fk :artist_id}))         ;#1
```

Notice at the `#1`, that we have to define the foreign key. This is because the foreign key doesn't conform to Korma's assumptions of `id` or `[entityname]_id`. Defining these relationships provides Korma with join information for the generated SQL.

# Constructing SELECT queries

Select queries are made using the `select` function, followed by an entity, and an optional body of forms. At its simplest, we can select all the records in a table by doing the following:

```
(select artists)
```

This will return all the columns of all the artists in our artists table.

Alternatively, we can restrict which fields to retrieve using the `fields` function:

```
(select artists
  (fields :artist_id :name))
```

This will return only the `artist_id` and `name` columns of all the artists in the table.

We can provide a `where` clause for filtering results by using the `where` function, which accepts a map of key/value pairs:

```
(select artists
  (fields :artist_id :name)
  (where {:name "Brant" :artist_id 10}))
```

The preceding code will select all the artists with the name `Brant` and an `artist_id` that is `10` (admittedly, kind of a useless query). If we wanted to select all the artists with the name `Brant` or the name `Smokey Fouler`, we could provide a series of maps tied together using the `or` function:

```
(select artists
        (fields :artist_id :name)
        (where (or {:name "Brant"}
                   {:name "Smokey Fouler"})))
```

Conversely, we can make multiple calls to where, which will "and" all the clauses together:

```
(select artists
        (fields :artist_id :name)
        (where (or {:name "Brant"}
                   {:name "Smokey Fouler"}))
        (where (not (= :updated_at :created_at))))
```

On our `recently-added` albums page, we return the ten most recent albums. We do this by using Korma's `limit` and `order` functions:

```
(select albums
        (order :created_at :DESC)
        (limit 10))
```

Additionally, we can join the `albums` table back to the `artists` table and restrict which artists' albums are returned by using a combination of Korma's `join` and `where` functions:

```
(select albums
  (join artists)
  (where {:artists.name "Brant"}))
```

This will return all the columns with only Brant's albums. Additionally, we can return some artist information along with each album by using Korma's `with` function:

```
(select albums
  (with artists)
  (where {:artists.name "Brant"}))
```

The preceding script will return all the columns for the artist named Brant, and all of Brant's albums. This is equivalent to the following SQL:

```
SELECT albums.*, artists.*
FROM albums
LEFT JOIN artists ON artists.artist_id=albums.artist_id
WHERE artists.name = 'Brant'
```

However, this can pose a problem because both the `artists` and `albums` tables have similarly named fields, such as `created_at`, `updated_at`, and `name`. The `fields` function not only allows us to specify which fields we want returned from the database, but also any aliases we want to give those fields:

```
(select albums
        (fields :album_id [:name :album_name]
                [:created_at :album_created_at]
                [:updated_at :album_updated_at])
        (with artists
              (fields [:name :artist_name]
                      [:created_at :artist_created_at]
                      [:updated_at :artist_updated_at]))
        (where {:artists.name "Brant"}))
```

This will alias the `albums.name` column to `albums.album_name`, `albums.created_at` to `albums.album_created_at`, and so on.

# Constructing INSERT queries

Inserting records using Korma is relatively trivial. Just call Korma's `insert` function and pass it the entity and a map of values:

```
(insert artists (values {:name "Maude Squad"}))
```

Be careful however, as Korma will generate an insert statement to include every key in the map. For example, the following insert query fails because the `:fake_column` key doesn't map to any column on the `artists` table:

```
(insert artists (values {:name "Maude Squad"
                         :fake_column "Will destroy you."}))
```

# Constructing UPDATE queries

You can update a record using Korma's `update` and `set-fields` functions:

```
(update artists
  (set-fields {:name "Carlos Hungus"})
  (where {:name "Hungus"}))
```

The preceding script will update all the artist names to Carlos Hungus where the artist name is currently `Hungus`. Much like insert however, Korma will blindly try to update any column name that you give it.

# Constructing DELETE queries

You can delete records using Korma's `delete` function. For example, we could blow away all of our artists by executing the following:

```
(delete artists)
```

The preceding script is something you're unlikely to want to use. Instead, to delete records for a particular artist, we could do something like the following:

```
(delete artists
  (where {:name "Carlos Hungus"}))
```

We can use the `where` function, as shown in the preceding code, to restrict which records get deleted.

# Using raw SQL

If you find yourself in a position where Korma doesn't support what you want to do, or where using Korma produces more complexity than the query itself (a more likely situation), you can use Korma's `exec-raw` function to execute an SQL string. For example:

```
(exec-raw ["SELECT art.name, count(*)
           FROM artists art
           INNER JOIN albums alb on art.artist_id = alb.artist_id
           GROUP BY art.name
           HAVING count(*) > ?" [1]] :results)
```

# Using transactions

You can wrap any number of Korma actions inside a `korma.db/transaction` form to perform a transaction. If anything fails inside the `transaction` block, then the actions will automatically be rolled back. Otherwise, if everything executes successfully, the transaction will be committed:

```
(transaction
  (delete artists (where {:name "Carlos Hungus"}))
  (update artists (set-fields {:name "Marjory Marjoram"})
    (where {:artist_id 100})))
```

The preceding transaction will execute successfully. Thus, any changes performed inside the transaction will be committed. However, consider the following code:

```
(transaction
  (delete artists (where {:name "Carlos Hungus"}))
  (update artists (set-fields {:name "Marjory Marjoram"})
    (where {:fake_id 100})))
```

Here, the `update` action will fail because `:fake_id` is not a valid column on the artists table. As such, the transaction will roll back.

 For a complete list of Korma examples, take a look at the detailed examples at http://sqlkorma.com/docs.

# Port the models from YeSQL to Korma

The following pages are what our `hipstr.models.connection`, `hipstr.models.artist-model`, and `hipstr.models.album-model` will be when ported from YeSQL to Korma. Note that the interfaces for each ported function are kept the same as YeSQL's generated functions, meaning that the ported functions will accept maps instead of explicit literals. If we were to design the model layer with Korma first and foremost in mind, our interfaces would have been simpler. The goal of this port is to illustrate how we can write the YeSQL-generated functions using Korma, and still have it work without having to modify the rest of the application.

## Porting hisptr.models.connection

Porting the connection is done by simply adding a call to the `korma.db/defdb` macro:

```
(ns hipstr.models.connection
  (:require [environ.core :refer [env]])
  (:use korma.db))
(def db-spec {:classname   (env :db-classname)
              :subprotocol (env :db-subprotocol)
              :subname     (env :db-subname)
              :user        (env :db-user)
              :password    (env :db-password)})

; Declares the hipstr-db Korma database connection,
; which leverages our already existing db-spec
(defdb hipstr-db db-spec)
```

## Porting hisptr.models.user-model

To port `hipstr.models.user-model` to use Korma instead of YeSQL, we will re-write the YeSQL-generated functions. We'll keep the function signatures the same as the YeSQL-generated functions.

First, include a reference to `korma.core` and comment out the reference to `yesql.core` (but we'll leave it in, in case you want to more easily switch back and forth):

```
(ns hipstr.models.user-model
  (:require ; [yesql.core :refer [defqueries]]
            [crypto.password.bcrypt :as password]
            [hipstr.models.connection :refer [db-spec]]
```

```
                   [noir.session :as session]])
   (:use [korma.core]))
```

Since we're not using YeSQL, we can also comment out the call to `defqueries`:

```
;(defqueries "hipstr/models/users.sql" {:connection db-spec})
```

Finally, we declare our users table as a Korma entity, and then port the two YeSQL-generated functions, `get-user-by-name` and `insert-user<!`:

```
; declare our users table, which in our hipstr application
; is pretty straight forward.
; For Korma, however, we have to define the primary key because
; the name of the primary key is neither 'id' or 'users_id'
; ([tablename]_id)
(defentity users
   (pk :user_id))


; -- name: get-user-by-username
; -- Fetches a user from the DB based on username.
; SELECT *
; FROM users
; WHERE username=:username
 (defn get-user-by-username
   "Fetches a user from the DB based on username."
   [username]
   (select users (where username)))


; -- name: insert-user<!
; -- Inserts a new user into the Users table
; -- Expects :username, :email, and :password
; INSERT INTO users (username, email, pass)
; VALUES (:username, :email, :password)
(defn insert-user<!
   "Inserts a new user into the Users table. Expects :username, :email,
and :password"
   [user]
   (insert users (values user)))
```

By keeping the interfaces of the ported functions the same as the YeSQL-generated ones, we don't have to adjust any of the calling code in the application. At this point, you can restart your dev server and use the signup form to create a new user.

# Porting hipstr.models.album-model

Porting the `albums-model` is a little bit more involved, but the principles are the same. We want to remove the dependencies on YeSQL, and then write new functions using Korma that match the interfaces of the generated YeSQL equivalents:

```clojure
(ns hipstr.models.album-model
  (:require ; [yesql.core :refer [defqueries]]
            [clojure.java.jdbc :as jdbc]
            [taoensso.timbre :as timbre]
            [hipstr.models.connection :refer [hipstr-db]])
  (:use [korma.core]
        [korma.db]))


; (defqueries "hipstr/models/albums.sql" {:connection db-spec})
; (defqueries "hipstr/models/artists.sql" {:connection db-spec})


(declare artists albums)

; define our artists entity.
; by default korma assumes the entity and table name map
(defentity artists
  ; We must define the primary key because it does not
  ; adhere to the korma defaults.
  (pk :artist_id)

  ; define the relationship between artists and albums
  (has-many albums))

; define the albums entity
(defentity albums
  ; again, we have to map the primary key to our korma definition.
  (pk :album_id)

  ; We can define the foreign key relationship of the albums back
  ; to the artists table
  (belongs-to artists {:fk :artist_id}))

; -- name: get-recently-added
; -- Gets the 10 most recently added albums in the db.
; SELECT art.name as artist, alb.album_id, alb.name as album_name,
;        alb.release_date, alb.create_date
; FROM artists art
; INNER JOIN albums alb ON art.artist_id = alb.artist_id
```

```
; ORDER BY alb.create_date DESC
; LIMIT 10
(defn get-recently-added
  "Gets the 10 most recently added albums in the db."
  []
  (select albums
    (fields :album_id
     [:name :album_name] :release_date :created_at)
    (with artists (fields [:name :artist]))
    (order :created_at :DESC)
    (limit 10)))

; -- name: get-by-artist
; -- Gets the discography for a given artist.
; SELECT alb.album_id, alb.name, alb.release_date
; FROM albums alb
; INNER JOIN artists art on alb.artist_id = art.artist_id
; WHERE
;   art.name = :artist
; ORDER BY alb.release_date DESC
(defn get-by-artist
  "Gets the discography for a given artist."
  ; for backwards compatibility it is expected that the
  ; artist param is a map, {:artist [value]}
  [artist]
  (select albums
    (join artists)
    ; for backwards compatibility we need to rename the :albums.name
; field to :album_name
    (fields :albums.album_id [:albums.name :album_name]
          :albums.release_date)
    (where {:artists.name (:artist artist)})
    (order :release_date :DESC)))

;-- name: insert-album<!
;-- Adds the album for the given artist to the database
;INSERT INTO albums (artist_id, name, release_date)
;VALUES (:artist_id, :album_name, date(:release_date))
(defn insert-album<!
  "Adds the album for the given artist to the database."
  ; for backwards compatibility it is expected that the
  ; album param is a map,
  ; {:artist_id :release_date :album_name :artist_name}
```

```
  ; As such we'll have to rename the :album_name key and remove
  ; the :artist_name.This is because korma will attempt to use all
  ; keys in the map when inserting, and :artist_name will destroy
  ; us with rabid vitriol.
  [album]
  (let [album (-> (clojure.set/rename-keys album {:album_name :name})
                  (dissoc :artist_name)
                  (assoc :release_date
                  (sqlfn date (:release_date album))))]
    (insert albums (values album))))

; -- name: get-album-by-name
; -- Fetches the specific album from the database for a particular
; -- artist.
; SELECT a.*
; FROM albums a
; WHERE
;   artist_id = :artist_id and
;   name = :album_name
(defn get-album-by-name
  "Fetches the specific album from the database for a particular
   artist."
  ; for backwards compatibility it is expected that the
  ; album param is {:artist_id :artist_name}
  [album]
  (first
   (select albums
           (where {:artist_id (:artist_id album)
                   :name (:artist_name album)}))))

; -- name: insert-artist<!
; -- Inserts a new artist into the database.
; INSERT INTO artists(name)
; VALUES (:artist_name)
(defn insert-artist<!
  "Inserts a new artist into the database."
  ; for backwards compatibility it is expected that the
  ; artist param is {:artist_name}
  [artist]
  (let [artist (clojure.set/rename-keys
                 artist {:artist_name :name})]
    (insert artists (values artist))))
```

```
; -- name: get-artist-by-name
; -- Retrieves an artist from the database by name.
; SELECT *
; FROM artists
; WHERE name=:artist_name
(defn get-artist-by-name
  "Retrieves an artist from the database by name."
  ;for backwards compatibility it is expected that the
  ; artist_name param is {:artist_name}
  [artist_name]
  (first
   (select artists
           (where {:name (:artist_name artist_name)}))))
```

Finally, we have to port the add-album! function, because the way Korma wraps transactions is different than YeSQL's. In YeSQL, we have to get a symbol to a transaction and pass that to all our methods, whereas, in Korma, we merely have to wrap everything in a transaction form:

```
(defn add-album!
  "Adds a new album to the database."
  [album]
  (transaction
   (let [artist-info {:artist_name (:artist_name album)}
         ; fetch or insert the artist record
         artist (or (get-artist-by-name artist-info)
                    (insert-artist<! artist-info))
         album-info (assoc album :artist_id (:artist_id artist))]
     (or (get-album-by-name album-info)
         (insert-album<! album-info)))))
```

If you restart your dev server, you'll find that the recently-added albums, as well as the artist and albums pages, behave as they did before.

# Index

# F

**file structure, Luminus**
about 12-14
handler.clj 18, 19
layout.clj 15, 16
middleware.clj 16, 17
repl.clj 19, 20
routes/home.clj 17
session_manager.clj 14
util.clj 14
**filters**
about 54
with parameters 54
**format-of rule**
using 66
**form POST**
errors, reporting to users 72-74
handling 61, 62
validating 63
validating, with noir.validation
    namespace 63
validating, with Validateur library 63

# G

**get-handler function 31**
**GlassFish**
about 186
URL 21

# H

**handler.clj 18, 19**
**handlers 23-25**
**hipstr application**
about 7
deploying 186, 187
deploying, as standalone 188, 189
deploying, behind Nginx 189, 190
deploying, with uberjar 187
deploying, with uberwar 187
extending 165
load balancing, behind Nginx 191
login form, creating 166, 167
logout route, creating 176-179

recently-added route, restricting 168
remember-me cookie, writing 174-176
user, authenticating 170
**hipstr.handler**
about 27
application handler 29
app routes 28, 29
initialization hook, defining 28
shutdown hook, defining 28
**hipstr.repl**
about 30
get-handler function 31
start-server function 30
stop-server function 31
**home page**
creating 51, 52
editing 56, 57
rendering 52
**http-kit**
about 22
URL 22

# I

**InstaREPL 79**
**integration test**
ring.mock.request function, using 88
writing 87, 88

# J

**JDBC transactions**
URL 136
**Jetty**
URL 21
**Joda-Time**
URL 143

# K

**Korma**
about 193
database specification, defining 194
DELETE queries, constructing 198
entity 194, 195
exec-raw function, using 199

## V

**Validateur library**
  dependency, adding  64
  format of values, validating  66, 67
  length of values, validating  68
  required fields, validating  65, 66
  reusable validators, creating  70, 71
  URL  63
  URL, for functions  67
  used, for validating form POST  63
  validation predicates  68-70
**validate-with-predicate rule  69**
**variables  52-54**

## W

**web application**
  dependencies  10-12
  generating  8, 9
**WSGI  11**

## Y

**YeSQL**
  about  91, 106
  getting  107
  transaction, creating in  135, 136
  used, for adding user to database  107
**YeSQL 0.5.0-beta2**
  URL  106

## Thank you for buying
# Clojure Web Development Essentials

# About Packt Publishing

Packt, pronounced 'packed', published its first book, *Mastering phpMyAdmin for Effective MySQL Management*, in April 2004, and subsequently continued to specialize in publishing highly focused books on specific technologies and solutions.

Our books and publications share the experiences of your fellow IT professionals in adapting and customizing today's systems, applications, and frameworks. Our solution-based books give you the knowledge and power to customize the software and technologies you're using to get the job done. Packt books are more specific and less general than the IT books you have seen in the past. Our unique business model allows us to bring you more focused information, giving you more of what you need to know, and less of what you don't.

Packt is a modern yet unique publishing company that focuses on producing quality, cutting-edge books for communities of developers, administrators, and newbies alike. For more information, please visit our website at www.packtpub.com.

# About Packt Open Source

In 2010, Packt launched two new brands, Packt Open Source and Packt Enterprise, in order to continue its focus on specialization. This book is part of the Packt Open Source brand, home to books published on software built around open source licenses, and offering information to anybody from advanced developers to budding web designers. The Open Source brand also runs Packt's Open Source Royalty Scheme, by which Packt gives a royalty to each open source project about whose software a book is sold.

# Writing for Packt

We welcome all inquiries from people who are interested in authoring. Book proposals should be sent to author@packtpub.com. If your book idea is still at an early stage and you would like to discuss it first before writing a formal book proposal, then please contact us; one of our commissioning editors will get in touch with you.

We're not just looking for published authors; if you have strong technical skills but no writing experience, our experienced editors can help you develop a writing career, or simply get some additional reward for your expertise.

## Clojure for Domain-specific Languages

ISBN: 978-1-78216-650-4          Paperback: 268 pages

Learn how to use Clojure language with examples and develop domain-specific languages on the go

1. Explore DSL concepts from existing Clojure DSLs and libraries.

2. Bring Clojure into your Java applications as Clojure can be hosted on a Java platform.

3. A tutorial-based guide to develop custom domain-specific languages.

## Clojure High Performance Programming

ISBN: 978-1-78216-560-6          Paperback: 152 pages

Understand performance aspects and write high performance code with Clojure

1. See how the hardware and the JVM impact performance.

2. Learn which Java features to use with Clojure, and how.

3. Deep dive into Clojure's concurrency and state primitives.

Please check **www.PacktPub.com** for information on our titles

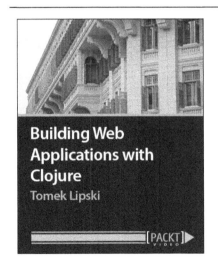

www.ingramcontent.com/pod-product-compliance
Lightning Source LLC
Chambersburg PA
CBHW060549060326
40690CB00017B/3655